# PAUL TAYLOR DANCE COMPANY
# THE DIAMOND ANNIVERSARY

This book made possible by a generous contribution from

## The Frank L. Ellsworth Family

ISBN 9781883285630  Paul Taylor Dance Company: The Diamond Anniversary

# A PEERLESS DANCE MAKER

After seeing *Speaking in Tongues*, Paul Taylor's stunning drama about religious hypocrisy in small-town America, Laura Shapiro wrote in *Newsweek*, "Only a great choreographer with the mind of a great novelist could have created a work of such imaginative breadth – a category in which Taylor has no peer."

In the 140 dances that comprise his collection to date, Paul Taylor has explored a wider range of subjects, and proven peerless in more categories, than any other choreographer past or present. In the wordless art of modern dance that he helped create, he speaks volumes.

More than a mover of bodies through space – although he's one of the best at that who ever lived – Mr. Taylor's dances show him to be an architect, dramatist, journalist, humorist, humanist, elegist, naturalist, psychologist, sociologist, storyteller and romantic, all in a non-verbal art form. While he may astonish us with a bottomless well of movement invention, with each dance he also imparts sharp-eyed observations about the human condition. The elegiac *Sunset* – one of the works that places Mr. Taylor among the great war poets – also exemplifies Taylor the romantic, the storyteller and, in its subtle suggestion of intimacy among soldiers, the psychologist, sociologist and journalist. The many-splendored *Esplanade* is poignant, romantic and fiercely athletic as it explores ineffable truths about relationships platonic, familial and romantic. "If you examined all its fleeting human incidents," Alastair Macaulay observed in *The New York Times*, "you'd have enough material to furnish a novel with multiple plots."

When he invited six friends to perform *Jack and the Beanstalk* with him in 1954, Mr. Taylor could hardly have imagined that 60 years later he would have a vast repertoire celebrated the world over; or that he would eventually lead his Company of 16 of the finest dancers into America's preeminent performing arts venue, Lincoln Center, on an annual basis; or that scores of his dancers would go on to found their own companies or become celebrated choreographers or teachers in their own right. Then again, perhaps he envisioned every last detail.

In 60 years, fewer than 140 people have been privileged to call themselves members of the Paul Taylor Dance Company. Many of those performers count the day they passed the dance maker's rigorous audition as among the most memorable of their life. They recall too – although memory can be an inconstant companion – the circumstances surrounding each dance created on them. Heather Berest has not forgotten Mr. Taylor's words on the day he began *Promethean Fire* in the wake of September 11, 2001. "'You are going to fall many times in your life. What's

important is that you have the perseverance to get back up again,'" she recalls him saying. "It was pretty moving as he addressed us with the exact words we all needed to hear, inspiring us to persevere through the inevitable hard times that life offers."

Other dancers notice things about Mr. Taylor that only his creative collaborators would know. Thirty years after he left the Company, Daniel Ezralow can still recall a particular Taylor quirk. "When Paul was creating with us and deep into his inner self, weighing the possibilities of one move or another, he would often stand up and try something himself," Daniel remembers. "He would blow our minds with his power and speed, but as he thought through an idea, I'd notice how delicate his fingers were and how they would do a little dance themselves, bending and arching and each connecting at different times with his thumb. It was as if through these small gestures I could see the workings of his mind. I don't know if others saw his hands the way I did, but I fondly remember watching Paul finger-dance through a creative idea."

Recollections of Taylor dancers on the pages that follow provide a rare, personal view of one of history's most important creative artists. On the Paul Taylor Dance Company's Diamond Anniversary, this book celebrates the Taylor repertoire and a dance maker who continues to move audiences as masterfully as he moves dancers.

Heather Berest in *The Word*; at left, Paul Taylor in *Option*

# PAUL TAYLOR

## BY ROBERT GOTTLIEB

Paul Taylor first came into focus for me as a dancer when he was with Martha Graham back in 1958, playing the swaggering, raunchy Aegisthus ("slimy," Paul called him), opposite Graham in her new and astounding *Clytemnestra*. It was great, she was great, he was great – the entire company was great. Those were the days of Helen McGehee, Ethel Winter, Bertram Ross, Yuriko, Mary Hinkson, Matt Turney, David Wood – an ensemble as yet unsurpassed, in which everyone stood out. (Maybe it was that experience which inspired him to create a comparable ensemble for his own company.) Paul, too, stood out in every role he performed – The Stranger in *Embattled Garden* (that's the Garden of Eden); Theseus in *Phaedra*; the Seer in *Night Journey*; and all the others. How could a guy so big and butch be so elastic, so subtle?

And then the year after *Clytemnestra* came *Episodes*, that strange sort-of collaboration between Graham and George Balanchine, dreamed up by Lincoln Kirstein, in which the two choreographers divvied up the orchestral music of Anton von Webern to create two unrelated ballets: Graham's about Mary, Queen of Scots, Balanchine's about the stark, atonal music itself. They traded dancers: Graham got Sallie Wilson, to play Queen Elizabeth; Balanchine, prompted by Kirstein, got Paul Taylor – and made for him an astounding solo, unlike anything we at the premiere had ever seen before. Twisting, coiling, thrashing, knotting himself up into impossible contortions – he was a revelation. According to Paul, he had been at a loss as to how to proceed until Balanchine famously told him, "Is like fly in glass of milk, yes?" It *was* like fly in glass of milk, although the fly was all in white and the milk was invisible. Paul performed the solo for three seasons but then was gone from City Ballet, having politely turned down Balanchine's invitation to join the company and dance Apollo and other important roles. The life of a ballet dancer was not what he wanted for himself.

What he wanted was to go on making his own dances, and with a company of his own. He had already created *3 Epitaphs*, one of his many collaborations with Robert Rauschenberg and the earliest of his works that's still in the repertory – that was 58 years ago. Soon would come the piece that skyrocketed him into prominence: *Aureole*, in 1962 – music by Handel, pure joy. It's still being performed everywhere. The following year he atoned for its jubilant spirit with the mordant *Scudorama*, with designs by another of his superb longtime collaborators, Alex Katz. After sleeping more than twice as long as Rip van Winkle, *Scudorama* was restored to us only a few seasons ago.

And then? Fifty years of non-stop creation. There are so many highlights it seems invidious to single out only a few of them, but one that has to be acknowledged is *Orbs*, that magisterial full-evening work set to Beethoven late quartets, which premiered in 1966. It was astounding then, and it was astounding when it most recently returned to the repertory, in

2011. How can anyone be magisterial at 36? But then Paul's work doesn't follow a conventional trajectory. He doesn't ripen along the usual arc of most artists. His pieces don't seem to belong to specific periods: There are youthful works made in his 70s, fully mature pieces made in his 40s. He doesn't date himself, he just charges ahead, full of surprises, expanding rather than evolving. He makes sure no one's going to take him for granted.

The range of music, subject, tone, approach is extraordinary. The horror of *Big Bertha*, the deep emotion of *Sunset*, the euphoria of *Esplanade*, the wit of *Cloven Kingdom*, the beauty of *Roses*, the charm of *Diggity*, the apocalyptic vision of *Last Look* and the elegiac vision of *Beloved Renegade* – how can all these, and all the rest, emerge from the creative impulse of one man? How does he manage to fit his movement so perfectly to such different music as that of Handel, Schubert, Elgar, Wagner, Stravinsky, Debussy, Offenbach, Bach – and the Andrews Sisters? Don't ask him – he won't tell you. His wonderful autobiography, *Private Domain*, of which I was the lucky editor, skitters and darts and delights, and even reveals, but it was never going to talk turkey about process. Paul is many, many things, but pretentious isn't one of them.

It's impossible to account for genius; you can only salute it. I'm going take a stab at expressing my view of his particular genius by cannibalizing a review I wrote in the *Observer* almost a decade ago – I don't think I can say it better today.

"Why do we love Paul Taylor? (Not the man, although we love him too, but the work.) There's the all-out energy and commitment with which his dancers move. There's the offbeat mind that finds large dance possibilities in such odd places. There's the unerring taste in music, in costume, in lighting. There's the way he accomplishes exactly what he intends, however obscure, while never forgetting there's an audience out there. (In other words, he's a man of the theater as well as of the studio.) But all that doesn't explain the strong personal connection we feel to the content of his work. We don't say 'He's so musical,' as with Mark Morris, or 'He's so interesting,' as with Merce Cunningham, or 'He's so smart,' as with Twyla Tharp. We give him not just admiration but visceral response.

"What is he telling us? Many things, of course, and that's part of the thrill. A choreographer like Martha Graham, in whose company he danced for half a dozen years, speaks from and to her own situation: Jocasta, Clytemnestra, Medea, Joan of Arc, the two Emily's (Dickinson and Brontë) – they're all Graham struggling to express and reveal herself. Taylor stands outside the worlds he creates: He registers everything – the glory of community, the dangers of community; the joy of living, the skull beneath the skin; both the power and the fragility of human connection – then shows it to us through a blazing yet impersonal prism. He's a loner looking in, rather than a volcano spilling out. As his laser-beam eye relentlessly exposes our nervous humanity, he smiles, shudders, sympathizes – not with *his* sufferings, with ours.

"Taylor the loner manifests himself throughout his career. One dancer may be set apart from the others – today [2005], it's often the prodigious Lisa Viola who, when she's not being the funniest performer on earth, or the most frenetic, can be a riveting still center, the eye of the Taylor hurricane. So we see her in the magnificent *Syzygy*, the most purely exciting dance piece I can think of, slowly revolving on the pad of one foot while, all around, her colleagues crash and burn. Then there's the mysterious dominatrix, the role originated in so many pieces by Bettie de Jong. She appears in the second section of *Esplanade* to modify and redirect the action; she's the Rehearsal Mistress in *Le Sacre du Printemps*; she's Big Bertha herself, that terrifying mechanical agent of destruction. Who is this outsider, whether benign or malign? A stand-in for the choreographer? By choosing so frequently to create such a commanding or commenting role on a woman, Taylor is placing himself at an even further remove from direct responsibility for what happens in his works: *That* one did it, not me.

"Taylor has been criticized for having a limited vocabulary, yet even as we observe, over and over, the tilting, listing bodies, the diagonal leaps and perilous slides across the stage, we come to realize that each ballet has its own highly specific language, from the happy minimalism of *Esplanade* to the tormented writhings of *Last Look*; that one baroque masterpiece like *Aureole* is different in kind from another, like *Arden Court*; that the Depression-era accents of *Black Tuesday* are nothing like the wartime accents of *Company B*, even if they're both set to popular songs of the period. In other words, a strong directed intelligence is at work."

What else has been at work is something that rarely gets mentioned in accounts of great artistic careers: an unflagging practicality. Its most important manifestation was his early decision to stick to what he knew best – and what he most wanted to do. When in the '60s and '70s he was offered Broadway shows, operas, films, ballets, plum teaching gigs, he turned them all down. In *Private Domain* he made it very clear: "Modern is what I set out to do and, come whatever, it is what I'm sticking with. Don't much care to branch out or gain a multi-faceted career. The key to success is the art of saying no. No to incidental dances, no to high-tech gimmicks, no to classroom situations. Best to concentrate and keep priorities straight. Career should not overshadow dancing. It's better to be career free. Be anonymous, just do the work."

He's been practical about his collaborators, not just Rauschenberg and Katz and other older designers but the great Jennifer Tipton, who's lighted almost every one of his works since 1967, and the brilliant Santo Loquasto, who's dressed just about everything since 1988. Why have change for its own sake when you're blessed with the best?

He's been practical in the way he's identified dance talent in every shape, size, and color: people come and audition and he scoops them up and grows them. He doesn't import stars, he nurtures them into being. And when they retire at the end of long and honorable careers – Carolyn Adams, Elie Chaib – or decide to leave while at the height of their powers – Ruth Andrien, Dan Wagoner – he may have private regrets, but he's ready with the next generation; we in the audience may go on mourning, but he's moved on. And since 1993 he's had Taylor 2, out of which have sprung Michael Trusnovec, Amy Young, Annmaria Mazzini, Michelle Fleet, Sean Mahoney, and more; he's always prepared for change.

He's also been practical in his choice of executive directors. From Charlie Reinhart back then to John Tomlinson right now they've been spectacularly hard-working, effective, and loyal.

In other words, he's protected his art by surrounding it with solid plans, solid organizing, and solid collaborators, never giving in to pipe dreams and fantasies. And he's protected himself by living a spare life exactly in sync with his temperament. He may have to go to a gala once in a while, or put up with the odd interview, but essentially he's either in the studio, making dances; out on the North Fork with his beach and his dogs and his carpentering; or contemplating the East River from the expansive windows of his new downtown apartment. (Beach, river – remember, Paul began as a swimmer.)

However he's managed to do it, he seems to have harmonized within himself the three essential modes of his work: the antic, the bleak, and the tender. We are the beneficiaries.

Mr. Gottlieb, dance critic for the *New York Observer*, edited Mr. Taylor's autobiography, *Private Domain*, and wrote the foreword to his *Facts and Fancies – Essays Written Mostly for Fun*. He is the editor of *Reading Dance*.

Lisa Viola in *Spring Rounds*

# PAUL TAYLOR

## BY JENNIFER TIPTON

I first met Paul Taylor in 1960 in the New York subway with my dear friend Dan Wagoner. I was totally awed by the experience. Little did I know that soon after I would be touring with the Company. I began working as assistant to Tom Skelton, who was the lighting designer for the Company. In a particular series of Taylor performances in three places, Tom could not be at the last, in St. Louis. The Company asked me to come along to be trained by Tom in the first two places and light the concert for him in the third. I showed up to start the tour in my Sunday best, including my fancy fur hat and gloves, only to get in a VW bus and ride for two days until we got to Chicago, where I had to sleep on the sponsor's living room couch. I was an afterthought and there was no budget for my hotel room.

Some time after that the Company was to do a Broadway season – I love the way that in those days we called four performances in a Broadway house, a "Broadway season." For some reason, Tom Skelton was not asked to do the lighting. After the season was finished I told Paul that I was happy to recreate the lighting of the person who had just worked with us, but that I would really like to do my own. He agreed that I should, and I have been lighting for the Paul Taylor Company ever since.

From my first baby steps as a lighting designer, to the accomplishments to my credit today, I have been guided by the eye of the master in my life. Paul is a remarkable, creative force. The dances pour from him – at least two a year – and each leads me to new discoveries and new challenges. I remember the early days when New York producers certainly were hesitant to give a full evening to any one choreographer because there might not be enough variation from piece to piece. Now I look with amazement at the tremendous range of Paul's pieces in any given program and wonder how it could ever have been different. I am not a critic or a dance historian but I do know that the constant surprise in each dance that greets an audience of Paul Taylor's is rare even today. It has been my huge pleasure to have been a small part of the making of most of them. It is rewarding to see the return of a piece that is years old and to be able to greet it like a friend – knowing, however, that the woman who lit that piece years ago is not the woman who stands here today, and therefore no change should be made unless absolutely necessary, or unless Paul rechoreographs some part of it.

Paul Taylor, more than any other person I know, has taught me that being an artist is as simple and as complex as living a life. I am so fortunate to have lived at the same time that he has worked – to have been able to share in this tiny way in the creation of the monumental work that is his.

Final tableau of "Brother, Can You Spare A Dime" in *Black Tuesday*

# PAUL TAYLOR

## BY SANTO LOQUASTO

Vandam Street was remote to me in the late '70s. Paul's West Village house was where we were to have many meetings, usually on the top sunny floor, a room I came to love, reeking of tobacco and burnt coffee, but that was part of it all.

The first meeting had been in the first floor parlor. I felt awkward and self-conscious and the more Paul spoke the more bewildered I became. The ideas seemed too dense for me to grapple with. I passed on it.

It wasn't until almost ten years later that I took on a piece, *Counterswarm*.

The sensation of bewilderment has continued on occasion over the years, but I deal with it differently now. It is often a more private struggle.

Paul's visual instinct is not only personal but invariably surprising. He is a true artist. It has been amazing to find myself trying to physicalize his impulse or at least punctuate it. The need to give him room is essential. The atmosphere can be created, but the story is yet to be told. What may seem naïve can in fact be menacing, outrageous and packed with complex meaning. The coy and the playful serve to cover anger and loss.

After many years together and even in the midst of frustration, we do press on. Paul has provided countless opportunities for me to reexamine the box we work in. He shakes it up now and then and for that I remain grateful. What I provide is often nothing more than a mere sketch, a cartoon, a shadow. There should always be room for others to complete the image and more importantly for Paul to take possession.

He has never been one to make it easy. And I thank him for that.

Julie Tice and Sean Mahoney in *De Sueños que se Repiten (of recurring dreams)*

# THE GREAT AMERICAN CHOREOGRAPHER

## BY SUZANNE CARBONNEAU

The idea of the Great American Novel continues to haunt the world of letters. Such a book would be a compendium of the American spirit, summoning all the feelings, customs, and experience of life. But is such a thing possible? Accounting for this mongrel democracy spread across an entire continent would seem challenge enough. But the writer would also have to contend with Puritan John Winthrop's declaration that "we shall be as a City upon a hill." Unmasking the failed promise of exceptionalism must be at the core of any honest assessment of America, as it is in the work of those authors – Melville, Twain, Fitzgerald, Faulkner, Nabokov, Bellow, among them – who have been proposed as the Great American Novelist.

But what of the Great American Choreographer? Is there a dance maker who has expressed the country's spirit in all its messy contradictions; who has delineated its culture and times with exacting specificity but also universal resonance; who has limned the tensions in democracy between community and the individual; who has grappled with the distance between America as myth and reality; who has analyzed the riddle of the national psyche; who has a feeling for nature as well as civilization? Is there a choreographer who has portrayed America, wholly and truthfully, as simultaneously inno-

cent and depraved? Surely, that choreographer is Paul Taylor.

Like America itself, Paul Taylor is self-invented. There is simply nothing in his background to account for his emergence as one of the most important artists produced by this country. Poet and laborer, he burst forth from the unlikely precincts of the working class to propose a new vision for choreography: speaking simultaneously as titanic artist and as vox populi. The fact that Taylor has sustained that vision for sixty years – and counting – heaps miracle upon miracle.

Taylor began his career at a particularly fortuitous moment. Following World War II, the center of the art world had shifted from the Old World to the New, and Taylor made his way to New York in the early 1950s to take part in that ferment of experimentation. He came prepared; his work ethic and strength of will were equal in ferocity to his talent. Before Taylor, American dancers had not looked like this: tall, rugged, muscular. A singular amalgam of athleticism and lyricism, his movement quality suited most any style or subject. Martha Graham proclaimed that "he has been chosen by the gods" and took him into her company. He caught the eye of Lincoln Kirstein, who brought him to George Balanchine. And he couldn't have been luckier in his timing: Graham and Balanchine had spent the previous two decades creating an

Michelle Fleet, Eran Bugge, Laura Halzack and George Smallwood in *Esplanade*

American audience for dance as an art form. With vaulting ambition of his own, Taylor meant to expand that audience on his own terms.

Taylor grew up during the Depression in a family that mistrusted art as the pursuit of intellectuals, a class for whom they harbored personal animosity. (When Taylor was just a toddler, his mother had divorced his physicist father, effectively banishing him from the boy's life. She declared that there were to be no more geniuses in the family.) And even though Taylor would find his way to art, he has continued to heed the essence of his mother's warning. Sensing that his gifts could be corrupted by artists' in-groups and the smart set, he has walled himself off from urbanity, bohemianism, and the social elite. Taylor cares more for the regard of the mechanic who keeps his car in working order than he does for that of the movers and shakers who serve as arbiters of taste.

After a start as an experimentalist choreographing for a coterie, Taylor chose to expand his craft and subject matter in an attempt to speak, with deepening eloquence, to the many. He meant his work to be encyclopedic of human experience, and he set about inventing a catalog of choreographic effects – vocabulary, voice, tone, theme, stance – to compass this vision. His aspiration grew Shakespearean. As did Shakespeare, he created Comedies, Tragedies, and Histories that appealed to the groundlings as well as to more sophisticated patrons. And he not only consciously balanced his repertory among these genres but also did the same for individual programs. His shrewdly calculated mixed bills invoke the fullness of life.

Taylor has famously remarked that he is a reporter, drawing the raw material of his choreography almost exclusively from eyewitness observation. He is a compulsive – and virtuoso – watcher of the passing parade. Stretching back to childhood, his happiest hours have been spent collecting impressions of people as they have gone about their daily business, unaware that they were under scrutiny. As he took their measure, Taylor grew to understand that movement is revelatory of character and motivation. ("A particular giveaway is the walk," Taylor has said. "Walks are like fingerprints.") His choreography rests on this bedrock belief.

As a dancer leading a touring company, Taylor had abundant opportunity to take stock of his fellow citizens. For the first two decades of his career, Taylor observed America from the passenger seat of a station wagon as his company barnstormed through one-night stands, and he came to know the length and breadth of the continent intimately as few do, save truck drivers or traveling salesmen. Everywhere, he took the opportunity to make a close study of his countrymen: waitresses, cashiers, country club members, motel clerks, gas station attendants, ladies who lunch, factory workers, shopkeepers. He anatomized their mannerisms, gaits, habits, reach, velocity, expressions, postures, and spatial patterns. And in paying such close attention to their gestures and movements, Taylor sussed out their dreams and hopes, their illusions and delusions. All of it has been fodder for his

choreography.

Taylor's penetrating gaze is allied with an imagination in perpetual motion, forever trolling for the telling moment. A good many of Taylor's masterpieces mythologize the mundane. *Esplanade*, perhaps the most cherished work in the Taylor canon, is such a dance. One day, while walking in his Manhattan neighborhood, Taylor noticed a girl running across Houston Street to catch a bus. With his choreographer's eye, Taylor was pierced by the beauty of her action – her avidity and spiritedness, and what seemed a bit like heroism – and by the apprehension that daily life is filled with such miracles. In concert with his hero Walt Whitman, Taylor recognizes that poetry resides in the bodies and experiences of our most humble citizens if only we are prepared to see it. For sixty years, Taylor has created dances that prepare us to do exactly that.

Dance is a fitting expression of the American character. Since its settling by Europeans, America has been perpetually on the move – restlessly pulling up roots, creating cities out of wilderness, building bigger and higher, then pulling it down to start all over again – in a landscape itself alive with transformation. As the first step in his grand choreographic project, Taylor generated a technique that emulated this bustle of human activity as well as the roiling continent itself: its rushing rivers, vertiginous mountains, wind-swept plains, crashing surf, and shimmering deserts, no less than its striving towns and thrumming steel cities. Taylor had a lusty appetite for space, which he consumed with an inexhaustible drive that seemed the choreographic equivalent of eminent domain. ("I can tell that you live in a very large country by the way you move," German modern dance pioneer Mary Wigman once told him.) Tearing through the ether has become a Taylor trademark, as has the generosity with which muscles carve space into rounded, fully three-dimensional forms. It is a technique that pays simultaneous obeisance to earth and sky, requiring that the dancer find connection with gravity in the lower body, while pulling upward in the torso and arms. This bodily split mirrors the characteristic duality – heaven and hell – of Taylor's themes. Always, every action is performed with prodigious commitment and courage.

In his early experiments with movement, Taylor discovered a paradox: it was the very artificiality of a larger-than-life technique that enabled his audience to recognize something that felt true-to-life. This revelation was important for Taylor's ability to capture something essential about ordinary people: Our inner lives are filled with drama, and we are the heroes of that drama. Taylor's valorous dancing echoes that vividness of self. This is what it *feels* like to be alive.

Taylor realized something similar about choreographic structure: to discern our own experience within the vast muddle of life necessitated spatial and temporal organization that cut through the cacophony. He forged a treasury of symphonic forms, modeled on the crystalline patterns of nature, that yokes thought and feeling.

A Taylor dance is instantly recognizable for the movement language he has spent six decades devising and honing, as well as for the glorious formal designs that he continues to invent and extend. But tone is something else altogether. Here, he is consistent only in his inconsistency. Taylor seems an artist of multiple personalities, often within the same dance. Desolation and joy, acidity and lyricism, cynicism and naiveté, corruption and purity carry equal water in his repertory. Observers are often unsettled by these clashing moods, and it is true that few artists make such radical tonal changes across their work. But for Taylor, these shifts reflect his desire to make dances that paint the panoply of life.

The most beloved works in the repertory are Taylor's rendering of the great American promise: All are equal, each person free to pursue happiness. Certainly, dances such as *Aureole*, *Arden Court*, *Airs*, and *Brandenburgs* speak to moments in our lives that achieve this ideal – the swoon of new love, the rush of high spirits, the conviviality of friendship. With their exaltation of concord, the dances also remind us that America has a long history of utopianism, stretching as far back as the Plymouth Colony. Taylor's sympathies are with the American ideal – the free and equal individual thriving within a circle of familiars – and he has returned again and again to this vision in his choreography. But we have to pay close attention. In a Taylor dance, there is always more to the story. In *Esplanade*, for example, so giddy are we to surf the ocean of communalism surging through its finale that it is easy to forget the undertow of isolation that had threatened to drown us in the second movement. Taylor understands that there is no joy without melancholy. As do the serious candidates for Great American Novelist, he never forgets the flood of despair coursing under the surface of happiness, ready to drag us under without pity or warning.

And then there are the dances that lay bare the American Dream as a chimera. *Scudorama* is the granddaddy of a series of works that indict lives leached of meaning by consumerism, conformity, and middle-class pieties. In *From Sea to Shining Sea*, Taylor gives American history the funny paper treatment, slyly exposing our founding myths as so much hokum. The deadly comic *Le Sacre du Printemps (The Rehearsal)* embraces American popular culture – vaudeville, Hollywood noir, comics, and pulp fiction – as the unlikeliest of foundations for philosophical inquiry. While the setting is cartoonish, the worldview is not. In this contest of good and evil, there is no winner. The universe remains forever disinterested. Innocence and love, depravity and hatred – it's all lubricant to that merciless mechanism. The world turns.

But Taylor doesn't stop there. In *Big Bertha*, we find him in deadly serious mode, exposing the hole in the American soul. The vulgar automaton of the title – corrupt at her core,

Ruth Andrien and Christopher Gillis in *Le Sacre du Printemps (The Rehearsal)*

corrupting all she touches – is America itself. There are dozens of dances, comic and tragic, where we see Americans in thrall to the carnival barkers, demagogues, and sanctimonious hucksters of politics, religion, and advertising. Taylor is anti-authoritarian and anti-clerical in his bones, and he will have no truck with cant or jingoism. He pulls no punches in depicting organized religion (*Speaking in Tongues*, *The Word*) as twisting the psyches of believers into denying their very natures. Politicians are equally menacing; in *Banquet of Vultures*, a president plays the ultimate con game, flimflamming a populace into war. Even the period dances, with their infectious tunes and jaunty dances, are laced with barbed comedy and excoriating satire. Keeping his wits about him amid the misty-eyed nostalgia for the Second World War, Taylor reminds us in *Company B* that a generation was slaughtered in that "Good War," and that America had asked her young men to sacrifice their lives while denying them the freedom to love whom they would.

And so much more. Conjuring the grand pageant of life, Taylor has been a poet of love (*Roses*), of mourning (*Musical Offering*), of carnage (*Promethean Fire*), of social commentary (*Cloven Kingdom*), of ritual (*Runes*), of war (*Sunset*), of sex (*Brief Encounters*), of the natural world (*Counterswarm*), of mirth (*Troilus and Cressida (reduced)*), of loss (*Eventide*), of average people caught up in the forces of history (*Black Tuesday*), of poetry itself (*Beloved Renegade*).

Taylor's achievement rests not only in individual masterpieces but in the larger creation of a repertory so vast and so varied that it seems impossible to have come from the mind of a single artist. When faced with the question of what kind of artist to be, Taylor chose not one thing, but all things: a sometime romantic, realist, editorialist, formalist, humorist, philosopher, storyteller, fabulist, and muckraker. Embracing the themes and concerns of the Great American Novelists – Hawthorne and Melville, Twain and Jewett, Whitman and Wharton, Cather and Fitzgerald and Lewis and Dos Passos and Steinbeck and Faulkner and Nabokov and Heller and Vonnegut and Bellow – Paul Taylor has given us the great American choreographic epic.

Ms. Carbonneau is writing a biography of Paul Taylor.

Andy LeBeau and Silvia Nevjinsky in *Counterswarm*

# 3 EPITAPHS

This dance was first set to lovely music by Debussy. Three girls who had volunteered to be in it were enthusiastic about their steps but when I thought the dance looked too pretty I replaced the Debussy with early New Orleans brass band music and changed the steps to lugubrious leaden ones. Robert Rauschenberg said it was either the saddest or the funniest thing he had ever seen and designed costumes with hoods that covered the girls' faces, at which time they quit and I had to find others.

– Paul Taylor

I met Paul at the Bar Harbor Summer Dance School in 1951, and then in the New York City dance world of 1956. I loved becoming an Epitaph. All the moves felt natural, a visceral delight. The opening always cracked me up – the jazz funeral band instruments trying themselves out and Paul settling himself in place. Then we ambiguous figments poked and lurched in diagonals down to the house of death. The first performances were at the Masters Institute of United Artists. Avoiding splinters, we wore ballet slippers, which also enhanced the black costumes, with round mirrors for eyes on top of the head. It was pretty stuffy in there, but worth anything to feel the connection with an amazed audience. The choreography had us stagger in sleepwalker-zombie earnestness, barely staying upright.

– Carol Rubenstein

*"One of the funniest dances anywhere."*
– Janice Berman, *Newsday*

# SEVEN NEW DANCES

We rehearsed in Paul's loft on the West Side. For one of the dances, each of us was kept to one small space. The movements were limited, the rehearsals concentrated and intense. Paul, as always, was a soft-spoken perfectionist. I was certainly very naive and never questioned what I was asked to do. But even I knew that these dances were different. They turned out to be as demanding and fascinating as any dance I've performed in before or since.

– Toby Armour

At the 92nd Street Y during *Duet*, set to Cage's *4'33"* (of silence!) a woman called out just before the end, "Louder!" Paul wore a suit; he stood just to the side and slightly in back of me. I wore a beautiful royal blue dress with a full skirt that fell in a circle around me as I sat on the floor with legs bent underneath and to the side, and high heels. I used the image of a group "picnic" to keep calm, since I anticipated the audience climbing on stage to clobber us. We also did *Rebus*, in which I stood beside Paul and in a flash, suddenly flung out arms and legs simultaneously in opposite directions – quite the opposite of *Duet* – the body riding the air for that interval. Thrilling! We later did *Seven New Dances* at Rutgers; the students yelled and applauded lustily, excited and enthusiastic. Wonderful youth!

– Toby Glanternik

After the first performance of my disappointingly unsuccessful *Seven New Dances* ended I went to my dressing room, where the manager of the concert hall was waiting to inform me that if I should ever rent the theater again it would be over his dead body.

– Paul Taylor

Toby Glanternik and Paul Taylor

"                "
.

– Blank review by Louis Horst, *Dance Observer*

# FIBERS

I was rushing to Paul Taylor's studio on 6th Avenue for a rehearsal. However, it turned out to be that and more; Rouben Ter-Arutunian, the costume and set designer, was at the rehearsal. There was a pile of slender telephone lines lying in a huge heap on the floor. The lines were of different colors and in an impossible tangle. We seemed to untangle wires for days. But eventually the tangled mess turned into a massive, abstract tree, the trunk going up from upstage right and tons of wires hanging over our heads. It was incredible. The music was Schoenberg, the dancers were Paul, Akiko Kanda, Maggie Newman and myself. I had come recently to New York from Appalachia with a degree in pharmacy. The abstraction of the music, the set and costumes, and most of all the movement hit me with quite a wallop! I had never been down this road before. I loved it!

– Dan Wagoner

For *Fibers*, Rouben Ter-Arutunian had designed the costumes and a gigantic tree made of the multi-colored wires that are found inside telephone cables. During the two days before the premiere at Hunter Playhouse, New York City, six friends and I attached each wire separately to the rows of pipes above the stage. The tree looked magnificent but was totally impractical to tour with. Later on, CBS-TV offered to air a duet version of the dance. The management insisted that both the tree and the costumes be redesigned because of the tree's impracticality and the costumes' "indecency." Although I thought the CBS designs really tacky, I reluctantly took the job because my Company much needed the money.

– Paul Taylor

Paul Taylor

*"Support[s] the choreographer's view that dancing need not have a specific 'meaning' to be interesting."*
– Selma Jeanne Cohen, *Christian Science Monitor*

# INSECTS AND HEROES

*Insects and Heroes* was the first time I was part of the original cast. Happily ignorant, I thought I could now contribute my own movement style, which was sort of flow-y and curvy, to Paul's choreography. I was so wrong. Paul was demanding of everyone, and although I thought I was doing what I was given, apparently I was not. My flow-y, curvy efforts were not appreciated. It was a major lesson in how to produce what is asked for and not interpret movement to my own comfort zone. With work and Paul's constant nagging, I managed to strip my mannerisms and achieve a cleaner, harder edge to the movement. Paul and I did a beautiful duet together. The milieu of the piece was complicated, mysterious and dense, yet clean and light. I spent the rehearsal period feeling like a squashed insect, but by performance time I felt like a hero, and a more versatile, better equipped dancer.

– Linda Hodes

Linda, Dan, Liz, Maggie and I trudged up to Paul's 4th floor, cold-water studio with its warped floor on 6th Avenue in the 30s; Paul lived in a small room in the back. I had a *real* part: I was the original bug, encased in a very hot, black felt garment, pierced from head to toe by nasty one-foot metallic spikes that extended outward in all directions. I was the foil to the pastel-colored leotard-and-tights-clad dancers, and I'd scurry around them in tiny quick steps, committing evil by hitting a triangle. This caused Paul to fall down and roll rapidly off stage with me – the bug – in hot pursuit. I reappeared to pull a checked tablecloth out of my ear, looking in wonder as snow fell. It was a fable – utterly magical whimsy – that I loved participating in. When Edwin Denby, attending a later rehearsal, told me he never imagined my "role" could be so well developed, I was pleased as all get-out.

– Elizabeth Keen

Linda Hodes and Paul Taylor

*"A delicious dream… And after all, how often is one privileged to gaze upon a dream?"*
– Doris Hering, *Dance Magazine*

# JUNCTION

We all had fun creating *Junction*. We were young and daring. We loved throwing ourselves around the studio. We lived on challenge, and Paul supplied us with plenty. *Junction* was set mostly against the music. Or maybe Paul was looking for different ways to use the music. Anyway, we tumbled slowly to fast music and rushed through slow music. There were lots of contractions; after all, we were still working with Graham, and the movement was very grounded. Several things no longer appear in the dance – the ceremonious folding of a checkered tablecloth, the unrolling of a dirty, itchy red carpet that revealed each of us as we oozed along the diagonal. The movement is still there; the carpet is not. *Junction* came when I was at a junction in my own life – trying to dance slow to fast music and vice versa. But for that moment we converged like a real junction, with all the possibilities that implies.

– Linda Hodes

During the 1960s, the Taylor Company performed with live music. We didn't carry an orchestra; instead, local musicians played the music. We performed *Junction* in London in 1964 with a chamber orchestra. However, one section had a cello solo that the cellist was struggling, unsuccessfully, to play. Finally he said to Paul, "This music requires a much better cellist than I am." Our good friend, the late Sir Robin Howard, came to the rescue when he called his friend Amaryllis Fleming (James Bond author Ian Fleming's sister), who was a concert cellist. Next day, she burst enthusiastically through the wings onto the stage and said she would be delighted to play for us. That night it was very hard to perform *Junction* because the music was so magnificent. I just wanted to stand in the wings and listen. We were truly grateful to her for her generous performance, but, interestingly, it was she who brought presents for all of us.

– Elizabeth Walton

Jamie Rae Walker, Sean Mahoney and cast member

*"Shows how quickly and completely Taylor found his voice.* Junction *is a manifesto."*
– Nancy Goldner, *Philadelphia Inquirer*

# AUREOLE

I had just left Ohio State when Paul invited me to join in the making of a new dance and perform it in New London, Connecticut. The dance was *Aureole*, and it has stayed with me throughout my life, performing it, teaching it, coaching it and loving it. When Paul was choreographing it, the movement flowed out of him. It was such a pleasure to be dancing to this beautiful music and to dance with these other talented dancers. I really wanted to dance it well; Dan Wagoner said, "Don't worry, Paul will never let you go on stage not looking your best." Being inside Paul's choreographic process was as inspiring and rewarding as performing the work. Rehearsals were a joy. And dancing with him was unforgettable. Watching him from the wings and seeing him leap across the stage in the finale was like watching an eagle fly, with such grace and strength.

– Sharon Kinney

In 1993, I taught *Aureole* to a company in China. They learned the movements quickly; more challenging was helping them understand the spirit of *Aureole*. Self-expression, which we call "stage presence" and the Chinese call "Western Individualism" (undesirable), was difficult to wrest from the dancers. In America, a choreographer chooses a dancer capable of expressing the idea to be conveyed, and the dancer is free to express his/her feelings while performing. In China, the dancers do only the movements given, which makes a solo boring and a romantic duet sadly comical. One day, I mentioned that *Aureole* was one of the first dances Paul made after leaving the Graham Company, and he was feeling very brave and free. In the next run-through in China I noticed an immediate difference. My translator whispered, "All the dancers are talking about freedom." Some of them, including choreographer Shen Wei, have since immigrated to the U.S.

– Elizabeth Walton

Ruth Andrien and Elie Chaib

*"An interestingly variegated luminosity of spirit that recalls fluffy clouds on Shakespeare's summer's day."*

– Clive Barnes, *New York Post*

# PIECE PERIOD

It was the second dance Paul choreographed on me. The first section used baroque music that had four counts of six, but Paul made me move 5, 5, 5, 5, 4. I had never done anything like that, and forget about dancing to the melody because you'd get too confused. He asked if I would mind doing the dance with bare legs, which was unusual in those days. Then he asked, "Can you stand on your head?" I said, "I don't know." So two girls dumped me on my head, and I said, "Okay, how do I get out of this?" Everything was so new. The second section was a hand dance based on sign language; we had the hardest time learning it but we finally did. I just loved every minute of it. The atmosphere was so different from being in a Martha Graham situation because we could laugh. It was wonderful to be choreographed into a humorous dance!

– Bettie de Jong

In the early days when we performed in the United States, we often performed in funky places, while outside the U.S. we performed on great stages and to live orchestras. Among my mementos is a 1963 review of a performance at the University of Illinois where I am currently a professor. Here, we danced on a high platform set in the middle of a gym. A curtain framed it, but each wing had only a foot or so before a set of stairs. I remember swinging around a metal pipe to break the momentum of various exits. Doing this during *Piece Period*, the voluminous skirt of my Elizabethan Ladies costume swept the playing tape recorder off its perch. It flew through the air still playing! Charlie Reinhart was nearby when the thing hit the air and, like a great athlete, caught the machine with such agility that it didn't miss a note. Thanks Charlie.

– Renée Kimball Wadleigh

Eileen Cropley, Bettie de Jong and Carolyn Adams

*"Entertains through superb craftsmanship and genuine wit."*
– Walter Terry, *New York Herald Tribune*

# SCUDORAMA

We knew soon after starting to make *Scudorama* that it was going to be dark. It was the opposite of *Aureole*; we were crouched over, in contractions, angry, menacing, running hysterically. Paul used "The Rite of Spring" while we waited for the commissioned score to arrive. Stravinsky drove us, as did Paul. Rehearsals were so intense that we'd go to a coffee shop afterwards to wind down before going home. One rehearsal, Paul gave us beach towels and told us to run around the studio, throwing them over our heads and slamming them into the floor. He eventually added that to the choreography. It was exhilarating as well as therapeutic. Near the beginning of the dance, Bettie, Liz and I slowly and sinisterly walked on stage, turned to the audience in a triangle formation and started pounding our feet into the floor. It literally pounded the breath out of us – and that was just the beginning!

– Sharon Kinney

*Scudorama* took several months to make. The first parts were set to Stravinsky's "Le Sacre du Printemps," but Paul then asked Clarence Jackson to compose a score using the same rhythms as "Sacre." *Scud* was set to premiere at ADF at Connecticut College. The score, which was sent by Greyhound Bus, did not arrive in time for the first orchestra rehearsal, and Paul decided we would perform the premiere in silence. Paul's darkest and most serious dance to date was met with laughter from the audience, which didn't understand it, causing one cast member to cry in the wings. Perhaps the earnestness with which we did the unusual and at times violent choreography appeared comedic, or maybe the audience knew Paul to have a keen sense of humor as displayed in some previous dances. I believe we danced *Scudorama* faster that night than at any other time. The original score surfaced many years later when the bus station was torn down.

– Elizabeth Walton

Sean Mahoney and Laura Halzack

*"A revelation – a blazing declaration of Taylor's talent."*
– Robert Gottlieb, *New York Observer*

# FROM SEA TO SHINING SEA

Martha Graham's sister took me to see Paul Taylor at Hunter College, and I fell in love. With all the luck in the world, I joined the Taylor Company in 1964. The following year Paul started a new, mostly gestural piece. Designer John Rawlings – known as "Bananas" – said, "I see red, white and blue, and stars." That's when *Sea* began to gel. Paul became a biker dude, and he wanted me to wear a feather headdress and a slip. Bananas and I got something cheap at a second-hand store on 14th Street and I sewed sparkles on the shoulder straps. Later, Paul said, "I want you to run onstage naked." I said, "What do you mean, naked? I can't do that – what if my parents come? I'll never hear the end of it." I wore a bra and panties instead. The last time the Company did *Sea*, Amy did it the way Paul originally wanted. Such courage!

– Molly Moore

Why we performed *Sea* in Tunisia I cannot fathom; it is such an iconic American in-joke spoof. We were, though, staying at an amazingly beautiful amphitheater/estate overlooking the Mediterranean Sea! In one section, Carolyn Adams had to sweep the stage floor. She had pre-set her broom backstage; when she went to grab it, it was gone! She frantically raced underground from stage-left to -right and found it in the hands of a local housekeeper-fellow, from whom she wrested it and resumed her part onstage. I loved doing *Sea*, especially the Superman/Lois Lane part with my ex-husband, Jack. He, as America's beloved superhero, would punch me in the stomach as I, starry-eyed and love-sick, followed him in my fringy red dress and high heels, tooting my horn with each punch! Pilgrims and Native Americans; Show Girls; Ku-Klux-Klanners; Superheroes; icons... no group was exempt from Paul's wicked yet good-natured sweep of social commentary.

– Janet Aaron Nightingale

Paul Taylor and Molly Moore

*"If the United States had a proper arts policy,*
*Taylor would be declared a national treasure."*
– Christine Temin, *Boston Globe*

# ORBS

When we started *Orbs*, I had been dancing with Paul for about six years. *Orbs* was a magnificent experience, I think primarily because I had been dancing with Paul long enough to not only accomplish the fiendish technique, but could begin to kinesthetically inhabit the structure of the dance. To live inside of the movement. And the movement was grand. Broad, expansive and evocative of all the grand themes – guilt, forgiveness and redemption. When I think about *Orbs* I feel fulfillment.

– Dan Wagoner

*Orbs* was the first piece Paul made after I joined the Company. I was so excited to begin. Disaster struck almost immediately. Danny Grossman and I collided and there was my little toe at right angles to my foot! I was out for the first six weeks of rehearsal. Carolyn Adams kindly stood in for me and danced my part as well as her own so that Paul would have a dancer to work with. Instead of learning my part in the first half on my feet, I learned it sitting down and watching it in mirror image. *Orbs* rehearsals were long and intense. I just couldn't take another step. When I got home I crawled up to my apartment on the third floor; I was just 23! At one point Paul threw out an entire week's worth of work and replaced it with the exquisite, quiet quartet toward the end of the dance. What courage he had.

– Jane Kosminsky

James Samson, Aileen Roehl and cast members

*"A kind of astronaughty tour of love and life on the planets."*

*– Time*

# PUBLIC DOMAIN

It was close to 5:30 in the afternoon. It had been one of those intensely long and exhausting rehearsals. We were all drooping when Paul announced that he would like to begin the trio. I burst out laughing. I didn't know how any of us could continue. "Jane, you stay," he said. "You too," he said, pointing to Cliff Keuter and Jack Nightingale. We began by learning a long and luscious adagio downstage left. Each movement had ten counts to it. It was liquid and lovely. "Now," he said, "I'd like you to do it ten times as fast." What took ten counts would now take one! I was afraid I was going to have another one of those exhausted *Orbs* moments when I got home.

– Jane Kosminsky

*Public Domain* was one of the first dances Paul made when I joined his Company. What I found most remarkable and invigorating was his uncanny ability to bring out the best in each dancer physically and artistically. The evolution of the dance was what the rehearsal process was about, but it seemed similarly true that Paul was deeply mindful of the contribution each dancer brought to the work.

– Cliff Keuter

In those days Paul worked with small groups of dancers on the different sections of a dance, so we didn't see a whole work develop the way today's dancers do. John Herbert McDowell was a brilliant musician and this score flowed beautifully even though it was a collage of works in the public domain. Paul took Carolyn and Danny to the Palladium to see some of the popular dances of that time – "the chicken," "the monkey" or whatever. Then he created a new movement vocabulary for *Public Domain*; it became a "dictionary" for later dances.

– Bettie de Jong

Eran Bugge and cast member

*"A delectable parody, a great, sophisticated joke."*
– Allan Ulrich, *Dance Magazine*

# PRIVATE DOMAIN

I remember that Danny Grossman and I were called in first and Paul began a duet for us. We knew there would be a score at some point but he choreographed it to the film soundtrack of *Barbarella*, starring Jane Fonda. The music had a buoyant, driving rhythm so we didn't notice that the duet was all in the air; no walking, running, skipping or stopping, and it covered the entire stage. When the Iannis Xenakis score arrived with no discernible pulse or rhythm, we all danced to the rhythm of swiveling hips, swaying arms and heartbeats, or we dallied with un-metered, self-indulgent detachment, hoping that a certain movement would coincide with a musical land-mark. When the set arrived with its three panels, obscuring much of the stage from the audience's view, I began to feel conspicuous.

– Carolyn Adams

Paul has me understudy Jane Kosminsky's part in *Private Domain*, and when Jane has knee surgery I jump into her role. It feels bizarre to perform a dance with panels that hide and reveal the movements of the dancers as we travel across the landscape. In the studio, at first there are no panels, so we must imagine the space (and the visual images in Paul's head!). Adding to the strangeness is the music, with its ab-sence of melody and easily breathable, countable phrasing. Thus, we dancers are challenged more than ever to be totally aware of one another visually, spatially and musically. The cos-tumes – shiny silver, skimpy, bikini-like elastic underwear – add to the feeling of physical and emotional vulnerability, as we are subjected to the voyeurism of the audience in this private/public, internal/external world of partially hidden eroticism. It is a uniquely creepy yet tantalizing journey.

– Janet Aaron Nightingale

Jeffrey Smith and Jamie Rae Walker

*"A disturbing resonance… that becomes a voyeuristic glimpse into clinical eroticism."*
– Anna Kisselgoff, *New York Times*

# BIG BERTHA

We were on tour in St. Louis and on a free day a bunch of us visited the Melody Museum, which exhibited turn-of-the-century band and nickelodeon machines. Big Bertha was the most impressive. Eileen bought Paul the LP recording of Bertha's music, which became the score for the piece. Cast as little Miss B., I raided my old closet at my parents' house and found my 1950s felt poodle skirt, which became the model for my costume. My father saw the piece only once and thereafter, whenever we performed it, he would smoke a cigar in the theater lobby.

– Carolyn Adams

Paul gave me outrageous counts and angular movements, but I was used to that. I was always exhausted after performing *Big Bertha* because of how tense I'd been through the entire dance. I knew if I didn't put every ounce of energy into the character – if I wasn't totally there and harrowing – that figure was nothing. I think that's when I learned to really perform. From the first step on stage, you have to be there. You can make the audience see you or not see you. Up to that point, dancing was more important than performing for me, and then all of a sudden I learned to consciously project. Carolyn knew how to really dance – I couldn't touch her in that department – but when I found something that I could contribute, I thought, *Hey, that I can do.*

– Bettie de Jong

Michelle Fleet, Amy Young, Michael Trusnovec and Eran Bugge

*"His bloodcurdling view of Americana [is] perhaps the best and bitterest satire ever choreographed."*
– Marcia B. Siegel, *Boston Phoenix*

# BOOK OF BEASTS

During the first years that *Book of Beasts* was performed I danced all the beasts myself – the phoenix, the squonk, the dying swan, the deity, and the demon. I managed to get through these exhausting solos okay but the real challenge was to change into each costume in time to make my next entrance. I particularly enjoyed dancing the squonk but its costume presented a problem. Seeing as there was very little light in the wings, it took a certain amount of luck to get my arms and legs into the appropriate openings. Guess wrong and I'd be wearing the costume upside down. This never happened but it easily could have. Years later, after I'd stopped performing, I thought it best to divvy my roles up between several different men, which seemed only humane.

– Paul Taylor

We wore black velour body suits and carried seven-foot poles. In the first section, called "Forward," we were in a line across the stage, poised balancing in parallel *passé relevé*. Quick, hopeful smiles and the lights onstage went to black-out, the curtain opened, and we were hit with full bright lights. Maintaining that balance for several measures was always questionable. "Forward" was built with patterns of marching backward, culminating in a double-timed diagonal crisscross from downstage to upstage. Brisk and furious, we just had to trust and go. Five of us brought Paul on as the Beast in a cage we created with the poles. Earnie Morgan knelt on one knee in the wings so Paul, and later Nureyev, could climb onto his upstage shoulder. We brought the Beast to center stage to escape his cage and begin his exuberant, hairy solo to the Dying Swan. This madcap medieval mayhem remains a comic delight.

– Britt Swanson Cryer

Paul Taylor

*"A sardonic suite that mocks human foibles…in thoroughly beguiling ways. A lovely, fiendishly clever dance."*
– Deborah Jowitt, *Village Voice*

# AMERICAN GENESIS

*American Genesis*: its first component, *So Long Eden* in May 1972 introduced me to John Fahey's music. Next, *Noah's Minstrels* in February 1973, that of Louis Moreau Gottschalk. I so wanted to dance those boisterous animal-like movements. Completed dance first performed in October 1973. Etched in my memory: my role as Gabriel, and the Brooklyn Academy performance. With full-length grey wool dress, halo and olive branch, I was the good guy who wanted to be the bad. I said so to Paul. His response – "Sweetie, we could have someone else be Gabriel" – quickly shut me up and I came to love the role. Opening night performance at BAM: a nightmare, and the beginning of the end of Paul the performer. Gravely ill, he carried on for the sake of the Company – falling, lurching, forgetting, we dancers anguished and fearful for him. Curtain down, season cancelled, financial ruin. But the Phoenix rose again in flame.

– Eileen Cropley

*American Genesis* premiered in 1973. In *Genesis*, Bible tales resurface in various locales and time periods in American history. *Genesis* belongs to that Taylor genre-within-genre in which, like *Piece Period* of 1962, geographical and historical contexts evoke metaphor. In my 17-year tenure with the Company, *Genesis* was the only piece I was in that I never saw from the audience. From a performer's perspective, I got a message I now pass on to my students: In one Paul Taylor movement phrase, a dancer can convey and experience the full range, from the minimalist gesture to the fierce, high-speed and complex. This is physical and dramatic information to be shared with our next generation. From the perspective of Paul's ongoing treatment of social and political issues and his storytelling of man's journey towards becoming human, perhaps the ultimate message is, "*Plus ça change...*"

– Carolyn Adams

Nicholas Gunn, Eileen Cropley, Ruby Shang and Earnest Morgan

*"Perhaps the masterpiece of American theater that wants to stand alongside that earlier touching and funny wonder... Four Saints in Three Acts."*
– Michael Steinberg, *Boston Globe*

# ESPLANADE

We knew it would be a dance like no other. Thrilling to rehearse. Counts, counts, counts! And ever changing directions. Mystery and ambiguity. Bettie sobbing while we crawled. Speeding feet and managing the curves with apparent ease. Tenderness and love in the duets. Daring falls and slides. Bruises, floor burns and body make-up to cover them so we can dance each night in "Nureyev and Friends" on Broadway. (Pride that Nicholas got more applause than Rudolf!) Walking all over Nicholas – my favorite part. Like a love bite, but forgiven while being scooped up into his arms. And leaping into the boys' arms with abandon. Trying to not look like a trained dancer yet being one. Teaching *Esplanade* to other companies and to Juilliard students extended the joy. And now, when hearing that glorious music and seeing the dance by memory – smiling tearfully. Thank you Paul.

– Eileen Cropley

We started working on the last section during the 1974 World Series. Paul wanted us to try "sliding into home plate" and asked some of us to come in early to try some different ways of falling. As the newbie, it was exciting to work directly with Paul and I became engrossed in listening to him…"Fall forward, now fall back like the wind is blowing you… Now twist and fall, okay… Rollover, good… Get up and run over there, that's right… Fall back on the diagonal, but look up this time." He paused and took a long drag on his cigarette… "Well, kid, looks like you got yourself a solo." I heard clapping and realized I was standing there alone while the others were sheepishly peeking out from behind the piano… "Better you than me!" Nicholas shouted. Paul could find strengths we didn't know we had when he made his dances, and even our limitations seemed to interest him.

– Ruth Andrien

Aileen Roehl, Michelle Fleet, Robert Kleinendorst, Jamie Rae Walker and cast members

*"A classic of American dance."*
– Arlene Croce, *The New Yorker*

# RUNES

During the summer of 1975 my Company was in residence at Lake Placid, New York, where each night Gerald Busby wrote and recorded the section of music that I would use the next day. We rehearsed in a gym where, each time I turned on the tape recorder, a multitude of common houseflies would entirely cover it – something I never understood and that gave me a feeling of foreboding. There were brown bears in the woods that surrounded the cabin where I stayed and I will never forget the charming look of curious detachment that one of them gave me, and that instigated using bear fur with which to trim the dancers' costumes.

– Paul Taylor

I knew nothing about a rune before Paul started the dance. The sense of mystery, power, goodness and evil piqued the imagination. And it was all in Gerald Busby's music – a fantastic piano score. I like drama and characterization and in my solo was able to stir the cauldron of spells and exit the stage with power. But nothing by Paul is literal, rather a swell of feelings to be drawn up from the gut. I also liked the "heartbeat" section when we all made a frame for Nicholas's solo. So simple – stepping sideways and closing to first position with parallel legs and hands on hips. Our bodies taut, powerful, aggressive and urgent. But oh! – the body pain by the time we had crossed the stage several times. I loved it.

– Eileen Cropley

Annmaria Mazzini and Michael Trusnovec

*"Enormous pathos… comes from the unstoppable energy of what Taylor has set in motion."*
– Arlene Croce, *The New Yorker*

# CLOVEN KINGDOM

*Cloven Kingdom* was one of those pieces you knew was going to be great from the moment Paul started. He had stopped performing but could still demonstrate the powerful bestial kinetics that came from his core. The process was non-linear. Paul quilted the piece much like the score, which was re-spliced on the fly. If not the first day, then during the first week, Paul called Nick Gunn, Elie Chaib, Chris Gillis (who was brand new from the Limón Company), and me into the studio to listen to a percussion piece by Henry Cowell. Two days later we showed the completed "Men's Dance" to the Company to cheers – not just for us, but the thrill of knowing a masterwork was hatching.

– Robert Kahn

As the newbie, I had ample opportunity to observe Paul's process when I wasn't being worked with: the duple motifs, people in groups of two or four, or two groups facing off. I was enthralled with the subtle vs. full-throttle movement. Here's what I got to do: split leaps slashing a swath through the action with tiny Lila York trailing; a full-bodied waltz in a glorious circular pattern with all of the women; a marvelously stylish quartet with all of these great torso twistings and luscious arm moves – all of this while wearing a big silver ball on top of my head. Two years later I inherited Eileen Cropley's exquisite gestural duets (with my idol Bettie de Jong), along with her shocking-pink dress and mirrored box headdress. But I also got to keep LEAP! step LEAP! step LEAP! runrunrunrunrun LEAP! step LEAP! step LEAP! … and I'm off.

– Victoria Uris

Sean Mahoney, Michael Apuzzo, Michael Novak and Francisco Graciano

*"There's so much movement-invention that it is hard to take everything in."*
– Anna Kisselgoff, *New York Times*

# POLARIS

In the summer of 1976 Paul was making *Polaris* in Lake Placid, New York, where we were going to show the dance as a work-in-progress before the world premiere in Newport, Rhode Island. My husband Don had been commissioned to write the score, and sometimes he was late finishing music for Paul. One morning at 5 Don and I were fast asleep and I opened my eyes to see Paul standing over our bed. He had started work early, as usual, and he said, "I need my music!" Don, who had stayed up all night to finish the score, answered groggily, "It's in the studio on the table." It was pretty funny to wake up and see Paul Taylor standing over me.

– Lila York

It was a beautiful summer in Lake Placid, and Paul's especially positive spirits infected us all. "Vicki, dear girl, you have no sense of style! Why don't you try making the steps I give you look good?" he quipped, eliciting giggles. Donald York fed us the music as he wrote it. Exploring the dynamic of lightness in part one of the two-part piece was a great challenge, as was projecting energy outward while constraining the action to the confines of the cube. Dancing a duet with expansively generous Elie Chaib was a pleasure. On one fateful domestic tour, the Iowa corn flu made its way through our ranks, so in D.C. I was afforded the rare opportunity of dancing both halves – the dark following the light. I also just have to say, those 20-something leaps toward the end, holding the arms curved up from the shoulders, were *killer*.

– Victoria Uris

Amy Young, Aileen Roehl and Eran Bugge

*"An interesting aesthetic exercise…that is one of Mr. Taylor's most beautiful [works]."*
– Jennifer Dunning, *New York Times*

# IMAGES

Paul was asked to choreograph a piece for American Ballet Theatre. He decided to make it on us, as he was most comfortable working things out on his own troupe. He started making a comedy to Schubert but canned it after a week and began again, this time with Debussy's "Children's Corner." The dance poured out of him, full of mystical images stemming from his interest in the ancient Minoan civilization. He told us of the women who rode bare-breasted on bulls, the visions of the Oracle of Delphi, and the society's adoration of animals. He made a wonderful duet called "Totem Birds" for Vicki Uris and me and asked us to teach it to stars from ABT. After 20 minutes of hacking through the choreography they declared it a no-go – too many counts and too many strange shapes! They sat down and smoked a peace pipe after that (Marlboro Lights, I remember) and the project was put to rest.

– Ruth Andrien

Gene Moore designed Minoan costumes with bare breasts. We petitioned for some sheer netting to hold ourselves up, and got it.

– Lila York

Opening night, spring season at City Center, 1978: On the first spirited head toss in my Cassandra solo, my wig went flying and landed with a soft "phuh!" center stage. There it lay, not adding anything good or welcome to Elie and Ruth's quiet, beautiful duet that followed. At long, long last, the next section began and Chris Gillis did a surprise turn, prancing out to fetch the hairy lump, his heroism rewarded by applause from the relieved audience (and me). My abject apologies to Paul were met with an amused smirk and a little pat on the rear.

– Victoria Uris

Annmaria Mazzini and cast members

*"Carries the feel of pottery shards, the dust of the British Museum…"*
– Allison Tracy, *Berkshire Eagle*

# DUST

The Company was on tour but Paul needed to get a head start on *Dust*. He picked me out of morning class, and we worked for a month on material. Not knowing me well, Paul came in with movement already prepared and demonstrated like a demon! I never saw anyone so big move so fast but with such articulation. (We all eventually came close.) Paul finds nobility in the capacity of the disabled to be optimistic rather than giving in to despair, and he conveys this in *Dust*. Most of the movement – fast, frenzied, and exuberant as it is – incorporates a useless limb, a crippled hip, and in one case, blindness. I had never moved like this before, nor with such satisfaction. Twenty-five years later I had the opportunity to reduce *Dust* for the six dancers of Taylor 2, and was grateful that I had learned, and remembered, every step.

– Susan McGuire

Paul created some very articulated phrases on Susan McGuire and wanted to see how fast we could do them. That was right up my alley! He also wanted gymnastic things, like a back roll into a handstand. Chris Gillis could do it, and I got really close, but when we all came in the next day and couldn't lift our arms up, Paul thought better of it. Chris and I did the back flips over each other, where I'm actually jerked off the floor and flipped in the air; I always felt very safe with him. Later, I'd have partners with different proportions or flexibility and some nights I'd think, *I hope I don't end up with a broken neck!* Paul said we were supposed to have afflictions, and the costumes would make us look like we had bubonic plague – and then Gene Moore designed gorgeous unitards that looked like impressionist paintings.

– Linda Kent

Laura Halzack and cast members

*"A fantastic new and macabre ballet."*
– Clive Barnes, *New York Times*

# AIRS

My most powerful memory of the making of *Airs* is of Paul standing directly in front of me, absolutely still, then slowly lifting his arm as if to bring the sun up. He was demonstrating the first movement of the adagio that does, in fact, bring the lights up on stage. The weight, amplitude and eloquence of Paul's simple arm movement told me most of what I needed to learn about the Taylor style. Paul described wind and water currents – the flow, the weight, the feeling of being under the surface of things, not on top. *Airs* is technically exacting, but the biggest challenge is to relax into the movement enough to convey Paul's intention. This is what I emphasize most when I reconstruct *Airs*, as I have several times for the dancers of American Ballet Theatre, who have come to love this sublime dance as much as I do.

– Susan McGuire

This rapturously beautiful dance offered an artistic vision that appealed to modern and ballet dancers, and audiences, as it was framed in classical music and sparkling costumes. There was elegant and delicious dancing featured in lyric swoons, expressive partnering and showy pyrotechnics. It was also staged on the Danish Ballet and wow – guess who joined us for a Gala performance? Misha (as I became friendly enough to call him). Yes! Superstar Mikhail Baryshnikov brought incredible attention to the Company and the dancing. It was a great showcase for Misha's talents and a lure to the "House of Taylor." I was so fulfilled to be dancing these dances that so well suited my dancing appetite, and proud to be serving Paul's vision, which had broken artistic boundaries. The work flowed deep into the dance community, raising all ships.

– Thomas Evert

Annmaria Mazzini, Robert Kleinendorst and Laura Halzack

*"A new and distinctive vintage, of a mellowness and classic finish that give it a sublime autumnal glow."*
– Alan M. Kriegsman, *Washington Post*

# DIGGITY

Paul and Alex Katz created a course of hazards by placing sharp aluminum dog cut-outs all over the stage. We also had a six-foot plywood circle that comically appeared as David Parsons and I managed to maneuver around the set piece: cabbage on one side, daisy on the other. I screwed up once and dropped the cabbage on a dog. But I was serious about this fun; this was a big break for me. Hot diggity dog – I was cast in a leading-man duet with Vicki Uris. The day rehearsals began I contracted "swimmer's ear"; it felt like I had a knife in my head. But this was not an opportunity I was going to miss! We performed *Diggity* a lot and the cast had regular replacements, which kept us working like dogs. This high energy, feel-good dance rocked to Donald York's music, but in keeping with the theme we spent a lot of time on our knees or in a squat.

– Thomas Evert

Twenty-five sheet metal cutout dogs duct-taped to the stage were out to trip or gash us at every turn, so we quickly learned to temper our customary abandon in their vicinity. Well, one tour (Asia, maybe?), one of those snaggle-edged pooches got his comeuppance and *somehow* got smashed flat to the floor. A bunch of us got a load of it during the "run around the cabbage," causing us to breach a performer's most cardinal of rules: *never break concentration.* To save my life (or my job), I could not have suppressed the laughing fit that ensued. But such a long time ago now... And still the mystery remains: Who or What squashed that poor little doggie? I'm liking the cabbage.

– Victoria Uris

Lila York

*"Taylor at his sweetest, with his broadest, slyest grin."*
– Jennifer Dunning, *New York Times*

# LE SACRE DU PRINTEMPS (THE REHEARSAL)

When Paul started *Sacre*, I wasn't officially in the Company. My first day, Paul created an intricate sequence of lifts with complicated counts. At the end of rehearsal, he invited me back the next day. What just happened? So much. As the dance took shape, every day was more – more movement invention, more storyline, more layering. The fulfillment of the narrative idea and the movement phrases fit perfectly with the arc and timing of Stravinsky's musical idea. That was masterful! To be part of Paul Taylor's brilliance was exhilarating. I loved the work on stage but it was in the studio that I was completely captivated. Paul was not only an inspiring choreographer but he was kind and brutal, funny and humorless, charming and a bore. How liberating! If he had the courage of his contradictions, so would I.

– Kenneth Tosti

*Sacre* was an epic for me; to watch Paul put all the parts together was thrilling! John Rawlings was the costume and set designer, and he was a bigger-than-life character. I remember a loft party (a lot of artists had lofts back then,) where John held court. It was wonderful to see who Paul dealt with during his life, these very exciting friends. I wanted that in my life; to meet other artists and to collaborate is very important. Paul had done a movement study for *Sacre*, a quartet called *Profiles*. It was flat, archaic, chuggy, angular, shuffle-y movement that felt terrible and was quite difficult to do; Ruthie called *Profiles* a 20-minute push-up. But as usual with Paul, it all came together. For the music he used a two-piano version of *Le Sacre du Printemps*; it was such a great idea to do that. The sets and costumes were minimal but perfect. And the choreography: genius.

– David Parsons

Michael Trusnovec and Annmaria Mazzini

*"A dance charade of ever so brittle, arch and waspish humor."*
– Alan M. Kriegsman, *Washington Post*

# ARDEN COURT

I was the first of this gallant band of men to burst onto the stage. We were a buff bunch of six who danced with masculine confidence and athleticism. Clive Barnes of the *New York Post* wrote, "This is the best male dancing in the universe." Like *Airs*, it appealed to balletic tastes. Parsons, Ezralow and Gillis had dazzling variations and I had what Paul called a "smoothie waltz" with Susan McGuire. Paul raised the bar and challenged us in the making and the dancing of this piece. As always he was digging and bridging new ground. We began with music by Greig but after a week trashed what we'd done and started over. I developed a knee injury and sought rehabilitation from the first generation of Pilates trainers. "In adversity is the seed of a greater benefit," so as I increased core strength and alignment it took my dancing to another level. My knee is good too.

– Thomas Evert

When Paul started a new work, the energy in the studio was filled with nerves, excitement and trepidation. Would I be the one he worked with privately, or the one he chose, in front of everyone, to focus on what wasn't working? Paul liked to pair me with Chris Gillis, a dancer of amazing talent and strength who radiated stability and trust. Maybe because of my wildness and improvisational nature, he thought the two of us would connect. We did, wonderfully. In *Arden Court* we worked on a whimsical, competitive cat-and-mouse duet that sped on and off the stage. Just as Paul had finished choreographing it – and we were both exhausted and pleased – he said, "Okay, now you both reenter from the other side and do the entire duet a second time – faster." It was totally unexpected and brilliant and it worked fantastically. The audience delighted to see us go at it a second time just as we had finished the first.

– Daniel Ezralow

Jamie Rae Walker and Michael Novak

*"One of the few great art works created in [the 20th] century…
exploring a new movement field of love and relationship."*
– Clive Barnes, *New York Post*

# LOST, FOUND AND LOST

When Paul first played the music for *Lost, Found and Lost* I was very curious how the work would progress. I had never danced to music that sounded like it should be played in an elevator. The first section was particularly demanding. We were all facing forward with no musical counts to rely on, only our own steady beats and breath rhythm. The dance premiered at City Center with an orchestra that sounded nothing like the rehearsal tape we were used to. It was one of those moments when we had to push forward and hope for the best. My secret title for the dance was "Beyond the Veil." Expressive body language was imperative. Costumed by Alex Katz, all the dancers dressed the same – veiled faces and black unitards – but I felt so special because I had one blue shoe.

– Karla Wolfangle

While most choreographers steal dance movement from a previous work, only Paul would think of stealing pedestrian non-movement. As the springboard for *Lost, Found and Lost*, he took the pedestrian positions from *Duet*, an "abstract" dance famous for a section where two dancers stay motionless for several minutes until the curtain falls. In *Lost*, I was initially lulled by Paul's satirical use of "elevator music," and I focused on the comedy by exaggerating the positions. But I realized the piece evokes a quiet desperation in the meaninglessness of the non-steps. Standing in line to mind-numbing tunes; standing alone in stillness with sudden bursts of "scribble" movement; jumping up and down interminably. In *Events II*, Paul discovered that even in the most objective abstract movement, the spatial relativity and motion of the dancers say something dramatic. I found that in *Lost*, the more one focuses on the abstraction, the greater meaning it has.

– Robert Kahn

Laura Halzack and cast members

*"Captures Taylor's wit at its most antic."*
– Allan Ulrich, *San Francisco Examiner*

# MERCURIC TIDINGS

Paul played the Schubert for us; the opening was seductively slow but it soon was off to the races. We giggled nervously because we knew we were in for it, and Paul had that Cheshire Cat look. He began with a lovely tableau and dissolved it until the stage was empty. After a pause Linda Kent was first out of the gate, embroidering the floor with her quick-footed run, followed by the rest of us crisscrossing like shooting stars. Paul invited us to use our choreographic prowess, *oy vey*. Monica Morris's idea was to hold a pose for three eights and move our arms up and down for an eight, but I insisted that we tear across the studio with wild, exhausting jumps. Paul was cagey letting us cook our own goose – he took those phrases and double-timed them. Monica has not forgiven me to this day. How the current Company can point their feet and maintain dignity dancing that first section, I'll never know.

– Ruth Andrien

*Mercuric* had lots of challenges, mostly because you had to be with your group of dancers – you couldn't do a movement at your own speed – and you were on stage practically the whole dance. Paul is so brilliant at traffic patterns: this group reveals this group and this group... and this was one of his most intricate pieces. My favorite moment was when three of us would run to three men coming out of the wings, and they'd lift us up over head. One night there was no one there – my partner forgot to come on – so I made something up. I was thinking, *Where are you?!* My last *Mercuric* was unplanned. Denise Roberts had taken over my part and I was in the dressing room while they were rehearsing on stage. Somebody came up and said Denise hurt her knee; she actually tore a ligament. "I guess I'm back in."

– Linda Kent

Michael Trusnovec and Amy Young

*"Young people cavorting with the kinetic propensities of young godlets."*
– Clive Barnes, *New York Post*

# SUNSET

My strongest memory of the making of *Sunset* is the feeling of hovering on the brink of the unknown. *Sunset* was my introduction to how Paul approached a new work; he didn't say much. The men were young soldiers going off to war and the women were their link to home. No one knew if they'd return. Paul said the piece was about the in-between time of not knowing. I overheard Paul and Alex Katz speaking about a photograph of young soldiers from the Spanish Civil War and the expressions on their faces of innocence and anticipation. Paul described the stark diagonal he wanted to obscure part of the stage from view and contain the dance in the remaining space. The "hovering on the brink" moment came for me when I entered down that diagonal and paused on an imaginary threshold of innocence and anticipation. *Did the soldiers see me? Would they join me in the dance?*

– Kate Johnson

*Sunset* was such a wonderful mix of artists who really worked well together. Paul knows how to pick 'em, and Jennifer Tipton, Alex Katz and Paul, with the Elgar music and those eerie loon recordings, just really jived, really worked well together. It made for a spectacular collaboration. I'm pretty sure it came quickly for Paul once he started; I remember it flowing out of him. I also distinctly remember standing house right at City Center and looking at all the components: the live orchestra rehearsing Elgar's music, the dancers moving onstage, and the set and costumes...and I just thought, *What a beautiful mix*. It's not easy to achieve, and Paul's the one who put it together. I had a very poignant duet with Christopher Gillis, bless him. We were one body sometimes. I just can't explain what that means, but we were.

– David Parsons

Robert Kleinendorst, Sean Mahoney and cast members

*"I'm always startled to meet people who aren't moved to tears by it."*
– Robert Gottlieb, *New York Observer*

# ...BYZANTIUM

We were still in 550 Broadway then, and the entire Company was called to work with Paul at 11am on the first day. He seemed excited because he'd had a very specific dream and we were to reconstruct it. The men and women were divided and put in opposing lines on shallow diagonals, and we beat out sets of rhythms with our feet. It felt so ceremonial, like we were speaking an ancient language. Paul was setting up a structure to be broken. It was one of those dances where I felt like I was in a tribe, like *Runes* or *Musical Offering*. I thrived on being part of the ritual.

– Sandra Stone

...*Byzantium* was a visit-to-another-civilization type piece, which I really enjoy. I love history, and imagining these places in that time. Paul conjures up these satisfying pieces that revisit the past: *Runes*, *Images*, and many more. I had a solo that went from side to side on the ground on one panel of the floor, sort of a repentant, flagellant, insect-type scene, and the floor was always clean during those rehearsals because I was just going back and forth. I remember how clean that panel was in the studio.

– David Parsons

Amy Young and cast members

*"Too gripping to be performed this infrequently."*
– Joel Lobenthal, *New York Sun*

# ROSES

I didn't realize the cumulative beauty of *Roses*, its simplicity and easy integration of many diverse couples into a seamless flow, until I left the Company and saw it as an audience member. I could not see the whole of the dance when I performed it. I don't think I wanted to. While I loved my partner in the dance and dancing the dance, it was the middle of the AIDS crisis; the glory of man and woman together wasn't front and center for me. With the passage of time, and the inevitability of change, I find myself calmly exhilarated and soothed each time I see *Roses*. A great dance, a work of art, can do that – reflect back to you new and different aspects of yourself and the world over time.

– Kenneth Tosti

"We can do it again – full out – no problem," we told Paul. "No, mark it – that's how I want to see it danced." Paul had just finished the choreography for the white duet in *Roses* and David Parsons and I were rehearsing together. What followed was a wonderful, thought provoking and, initially, unsettling experience. Fuller, deeper, stronger with the "Taylor torso" is the direction a dancer often takes – sending the energy out to the back wall of the theater and beyond. This time Paul flipped the most often used trajectory of a dance. All the "big" movement happens in the main body of the work, which ends quietly with the white duet. "Less is more" was the challenge – developing the role with all the richness it deserves but without using the tools most often chosen. It wasn't just a question of subtlety but of finding a totally different physical approach, presenting us with a new and enriching challenge.

– Cathy McCann

Eran Bugge and Michael Trusnovec

*"An ode to tenderness [that] blooms like a flower."*
– Anna Kisselgoff, *New York Times*

# LAST LOOK

On that first day Paul gently plugged us into an invisible socket that caused our bodies to shake, to shudder and shiver all over as if possessed. I don't remember him asking us to do it, rather I looked over and one of the dancers was already shaking, and then the move spread through the room like wildfire. *Last Look* was jolted into life by that ferociously articulate movement, with Paul deftly manipulating phrases we had come up with and adding his own to the choreographic brew. We kicked the air, spines lashing, threw ourselves into space like broken marionettes, then rolled on the floor as if our clothes were on fire. It was St. Vitus' Dance in a small studio in Manhattan in 1985. At day's end Paul beamed and we all glistened as if newborn. Next morning our necks were so sore we couldn't turn our heads. I wouldn't have missed it for the world.

– Douglas Wright

The dance is about looking in the mirror and confronting one's demons. My role – the woman in the pink dress – required a lot of pelvic thrusts back and forth. When he was making the dance, the thing Paul kept telling me, rather adamantly, about my role was, "It's all about ****ing." I was just 22 and I thought, *Maybe he thinks I don't know anything about this.* Then I wondered if I needed to go home and practice! When *Last Look* was finished, Paul's former dancer Pina Bausch came to watch a rehearsal. At the end of this apocalyptic piece, she very quietly said "Thank you."

– Raegan Wood

Michelle Fleet and cast members

*"A frightening vision of urban apocalypse."*
– Martha Duffy, *Time*

# MUSICAL OFFERING

Paul showed us pictures of sculptures from a primitive tribe in New Guinea: figures squatting in wide postures with bent arms and legs connected like strings of paper dolls. These were the shapes we moved in, as if carving our own effigies out of the earth. I was the figure who started the dance. Moving jerkily and slowly as if animated by an unseen force, I brought the other dancers on stage. The tension between the baroque musical structure and the primitive, abstract form of the dance was like being part of Paul's creative mind. I can still feel the mind meld we all shared, puppets to the great Puppeteer. In the latter part of the dance Christopher Gillis and I danced a duet that felt as if we were joined like Siamese twins; at the end he puts my hand on his heart before I leave. A masterpiece like *Musical Offering* lives on in you forever.

– Kate Johnson

A masterpiece; one of my favorite dances. The architecture and musicality are incredible and it's so much fun to dance! I had just joined the Company and was very nervous. Inspired by a Polynesian statue, Paul used the marvelous Chris Gillis to develop the movement vocabulary. Originally I danced a trio with Linda Kent and Doug Wright. Then I had to dance David Parsons's solo, very difficult for me – I don't think I was very good at – till I left the Company. Chris and Kate were just mesmerizing. I had my most embarrassing moment ever on stage in *Musical Offering*. At one point the whole Company except for Kate tilts from one leg to the other with arms doing an "8" shape, and I started with the wrong leg. As I tried to correct it, I made it worse, my arms going against my legs instead of with them. The longest 12 counts of my life.

– Joao Mauricio

Eran Bugge

*"One of the most extraordinarily reverberant dances of our time...*
*flows with uncommon ceremonial splendor."*
– Allan Ulrich, *San Francisco Examiner*

# SYZYGY

*Syzygy* is an alignment of three celestial objects; here the alignment was between Jim Karr's dancer quality, dance-maker Paul Taylor and the Company. Heavenly Jim was graceful, agile, lithe, loose-jointed, supple yet surefooted. The choreography and use of improvisation reflected Jim's organic dancing with a wiggly softness. Paul's creation has a celestial appearance with calm and frenetic swirling to Donald York's score of electronic, energetic sound. Solos have a structure but dancers are left to improvise and go wild, circled by shooting star-like dancers leaping. My favorite performances were in amphitheaters of Greece and Israel, under the stars.

– Constance Dinapoli

Flailing arms and bodies moving uncontrollably to music that was as far from Bach as you could get. As an apprentice, I studied from the sidelines, hoping no one would notice I was there. Apprentices rarely stepped in during a season, but Paul called one Friday. "I need you to step into *Syzygy* this Sunday; there will be one rehearsal onstage." I remember bumping into Linda Kent; other than that, I was a dancer among dancers. Paul, Jeff Waddlington and Douglas Wright made it a point to congratulate me after the performance. It was one of the greatest moments of my time with PTDC.

– Manuel Rodriguez

Paul was choreographing the last section. He told me to enter upstage left with a leaping turn and continue doing so around the group on stage, ending downstage left with "a big jump of some sort." After landing I was to rejoin the group. I vividly remember careening dangerously close to those I passed on my way to lifting myself into space with all my might in an attempt to defeat gravity for as long as I possibly could. It was simply thrilling.

– Barry Wizoreck

Orion Duckstein, Michael Trusnovec, Michael Apuzzo, Sean Mahoney and Francisco Graciano

*"A major piece of movement invention – a ferocious outpouring of energy…"*
– Anna Kisselgoff, *New York Times*

# BRANDENBURGS

Paul started choreographing it while we were dancing at the State Theater, in the American Music Festival organized by New York City Ballet. Inspired by all the classic ballet there, he started creating very complicated steps. It was not a pleasant rehearsal period. I think when Paul used to choreograph his "pretty" ballets he was much more difficult than when he created his dark ones, which I really love. It went through many changes and turned out to be a beautiful piece, very fun to dance. Working with Paul was intimidating and sometimes could be difficult but I love having had the luck and opportunity to work with him. It was a great time. I loved and admired the Company of dancers I joined; they were outstanding. I truly love and respect Paul – his calling me "Brazil nut" in the good times, and being the deadly pi-raña when his patience was short.

– Joao Mauricio

Paul has a reputation as one of the most musical of chore-ographers; this was one of the things I was looking forward to most when I was hired. Before he made *Brandenburgs*, I didn't realize that his musicality is instinctual; he listens to music and devises a personal "score" from which to create. I had played some of the Brandenburg Concerti as a double bassist, and as Paul called out his counts for steps, I felt like I was in an alternate universe. There were threes, fours, eights, and perhaps some sixes, but nothing that matched the score in my head. I looked to see how the other dancers were react-ing to this "score"; everyone went along with it. That's when I realized that musicality isn't necessarily something written in a score, but a wonderful, instinctual and playful dance full of possibilities. Paul's counts may not have been Bach's, but they were unique, honest, and truly thoughtful.

– Joseph Bowie

Michael Apuzzo, Sean Mahoney, George Smallwood, Robert Kleinendorst, James Samson and Parisa Khobdeh

*"Beauty is the only word for Brandenburgs."*
– Mary Clarke, *Manchester Guardian*

# DANBURY MIX

What a fun dance! Was I the Statue of Liberty? *The Times of London* wrote of my performance, "Part priestess, part cocktail party hostess." I was all of the above. The best was a high-tail run that made a loop into a flying jump, straddling my partner, knocking us into the wing and disappearing off stage. I pictured myself as Olive Oyl running to Popeye.

– Karla Wolfangle

While our physical input was always appreciated and often encouraged, Paul often kept the emotional context of a dance to himself. He has a unique ability to blend a classical sensibility with chaos and surprise; like a master comedian he'll set up a joke or story and end with an unusual twist (pun intended). The dancers would add or finish a phrase as if reading his mind. One day in creative for *Danbury*, Jeff Wadlington, Francie Huber and I were to do an upstage crossover. Paul asked us to create a phrase that changed elevation and tempo. When he returned 15 minutes later, Jeff demonstrated first. He leaped up, landed on his head, spun around, crashed to his knees and did some other painful moves before coming to a painful stop. Paul was impressed and had Jeff demonstrate it two more times; each time it was more painful to watch. Francie and I decided to kill Jeff if *we* had to do it.

– Raymond Kurshals

Laura Halzack, Robert Kleinendorst and cast members

*"Imagery of lacerating power and baleful wit."*
– Allan Ulrich, *San Francisco Examiner*

# SPEAKING IN TONGUES

The trick was to make the preacher both sympathetic and dislikable (one type of contradiction that occurs in many of my dances.) In the role of the preacher, Elie Chaib did a fabulous job, both on stage and in Matthew Diamond's film for PBS. Indeed, Elie has become a fable himself to Company members who never saw him perform.

– Paul Taylor

I was beginning my second year with the Company. Paul had already produced what seemed a lifetime of accomplishments, but this would be the only time he created four pieces in one year. I headed into the studio one beautiful fall morning just in time to cross paths with Paul. He was in a wheelchair being rushed to the hospital because of an ulcer. I looked at him with a scared, little-girl face for which he showed little patience. He whispered, "Just go on with rehearsal, Francie." He seemed to be in a darkness larger than his ulcer. Fortunately for all of us, he returned physically on the upswing, but it was clear he was still struggling, fighting through his pain and his demons. Step by step, his genius flowered into *Speaking in Tongues*. His courage and fortitude set an example for all of us. Artistry requires just that – great personal sacrifice.

– Francie Huber Mourad

James Samson, Sean Mahoney, Michael Novak, Michael Apuzzo and cast women

*"Illuminates the scary underside of America's most cherished definition of itself: one nation, under God."*
– Laura Shapiro, *Newsweek*

# COMPANY B

At a fundraising gala in 1990, a seed was planted. An exuberant polka began; I grabbed the other ballroom expert in the Company, Francie Huber. "1-2-3-and..." we went around the floor. People noticed and cheered. (Us: big smiles.) During the second lap, a few patrons cleared the floor to watch. (Us: bigger smiles.) During the third lap the entire floor cleared. We were glorious, basking in the attention and oblivious to anything but the "big circle." Watching us from the start was Paul, with the biggest smile I've ever seen – a sincere look of pleasure. The next rehearsal, Francie and I were called in. Paul put on the Andrews Sisters' "Pennsylvania Polka." The popular music maestro strikes again! He wanted to see a BIG circle (of course). That circle gave me life, and for the next six weeks it would give me pain, the good kind. Thirteen years later, with two platinum hips, I'd gladly weather that pain over and over again.

– Hernando Cortez

Company B was the first time Paul created a dance using pop songs with lyrics. He wanted to make a dance for the less senior members of his Company; he was beginning to see things in each of us that could inspire new work, so it was the start of a life-changing period for most of us. We were struggling under the weight of the AIDS crisis, and Paul could address the similarities of our different generations through Company B. I remember most fondly Paul sharing anecdotal viewpoints on what society felt like during the war-torn 1940s, long before any of us were born – the world of the Andrews Sisters' songs. The subtext and shadows of that world were relevant to us. And the timelessness of the dance was proven by its success among audiences of vastly different ages and experiences. The depth of our relationships and future work with Paul emerged from that very heady brew.

– David Grenke

Parisa Khobdeh and cast members

*"Evokes the exuberant rhythms of the '40s
as well as the grim and persistent shadow of war."*
– Laura Shapiro, *Newsweek*

# SPINDRIFT

A gift and punishment at the same time. Paul said, "The challenge for you and me in this dance is I am going to keep you onstage the entire time." Then, after two movements I was off-stage thinking, *What did I do wrong?* The dance is about being a loner and going your own way. Sometimes Paul had me stand onstage while everyone danced around me. Challenging me to fill stillness with movement. At one point he said, "Go over there and turn." So every day I did a different set of turns until after one run-through he said, "Do that one," and that's the one we kept. The solo he gave me was very hard. It was long, the turns were slow, I had to lean forward, touch my head to my shin in attitude and then promenade (turn) slowly. Ughhh. Making a dance with Paul, however, is truly a gift from the art gods.

– Andrew Asnes

*Spindrift* illustrated the interior process of Paul Taylor – fragments of thoughts, images, ideas, intuitively linked but unable to be articulated to the cast enlisted to complete the transformation to stage. To counter this, Paul came in with a notepad of counts and a set of rules that provided a framework that would enable us to meet the inevitable deadlines that were a very real part of his world. These rules would at some mystical moment in the rehearsal process be relinquished in exchange for inspired new work. The muse had entered the room and the catalytic moment that would propel Paul to complete the piece had begun. Paul shifted from a director of work to a willing participant in a chase to the end.

– David Grenke

Annmaria Mazzini, Michael Trusnovec and Robert Kleinendorst

*"Suffused with the very lyricism… which had always marked him out like some special child of the gods."*
– Clive Barnes, *New York Post*

49

# A FIELD OF GRASS

Following a layoff, I was driving back from the Adirondacks. Harry Nilsson was playing on the radio – he had just died. They played "Mother Nature's Son"; I hadn't heard his rendition, and I remember sitting back and loving it. When we returned to the studio, Paul had scrapped a piece of music we were working with and decided to start over – with Harry Nilsson. We started on the opening solo and it was one of those wonderful experiences when things just clicked. I liked the movement, he liked what I was doing and we did quite a bit before he even turned on the music. Then he put on "Mother Nature's Son" and I almost wept. It was a perfect experience working on that dance. Paul let me be who I was, always, even when I didn't know who I was myself.

– Patrick Corbin

The duet was the third or fourth time Paul brought Patrick and me into the studio for the creative process, and I felt very comfortable. We counted the music and began. Paul asked Dan Wagoner, who was visiting, for his thoughts; the section where Patrick and I jump over each other was Dan's suggestion. I was particularly influenced by Nilsson's "I Guess The Lord Must Be In New York City." You always need to have a conceptual take on the music Paul's using but in this particular piece, I felt the music offered me a characterization of my part – a young woman coming to New York with no money, no job, just the love of her friends to guide her through those first moments as a "New Yorker." Exactly the way I felt as a young student attending the first class ever given at The Taylor School by Carolyn Adams in the summer of 1983. I was on my way.

– Denise Roberts Hurlin

Michelle Fleet and Patrick Corbin

*"A stunningly succinct recreation of the apocalyptic 1960s and the decade's appetite for love, death and drugs."*
– Jennifer Dunning, *New York Times*

# FUNNY PAPERS

Working on *Funny Papers* was an extraordinarily rich experience. Dance provided the agency for Paul to speak, teach and mentor, and *Funny Papers* was the vehicle for his cautious support of my pursuit of choreography – a path he knew to be fraught with challenging and rewarding experiences. Pulling apart my work to formulate it into something new and unlike the original likely wouldn't have happened with anyone but Paul. He gave me that sacred place to try and to fail: his studio. I treasure that he mentored me by entering into my work, taking what seemed sacred and precious and allowing me to discover that it was neither. I always loved that Paul's work was fearless and the body was something to serve the vision of the choreographer. Paul continues to change and evolve what we consider to be even his most sacred works. *Funny Papers* enabled me to experience this fearless approach to making dance.

– David Grenke

This dance was unconventional from the start. Some of the dancers were choreographing independent projects at the time. *Funny Papers* would employ themes, quotes or material from these works, which would be set to music of Paul's choosing, and edited and cast by him. I was selected to be in a duet with and by Patrick Corbin. We put together a fast-moving duet to music other than would ultimately be used; very modern and edgy. We showed it to Paul and he basically scrapped it. We then put together what would become the "I Like Bananas" section, and I was outnumbered by choreographers! It was surprising to see the original work of my peers put through crazy permutations and turned inside-out. Whew! It all eventually came together, of course. I'll never forget the first time we got into the theater to premiere it – the strobing effect of Santo's half-white, half-black costumes was amazing to see for the first time.

– Thomas Patrick

Richard Chen See, Robert Kleinendorst and Michael Trusnovec

*"So comic in its intensity that it would be a grave mistake
to consider it only lighthearted."*
– Anna Kisselgoff, *New York Times*

# OFFENBACH OVERTURES

I liked performing *Offenbach* even though it was a "shoe" dance, and I had to work so much harder for traction and propulsion against the floor. It evolved, as all good Taylor dances do, into a real physical dialogue among the dancers on stage, with room for personal artistry. Paul was adamant about not "acting" or faking emotion. He'd see what was happening with the relationships during the creation of a work, and expertly craft movement and gesture to produce the emotion or story he meant to convey. And he'd notice things while we improvised and work those into a tapestry uniquely his own. Paul's choreographic structures are so well crafted that they support a freedom of artistic expression that's quite rare in dance. That structure supported the reality of who I was in a particular role, and I was able to live it anew – and nuance it in relation to a particular audience – each time I danced it.

– Caryn Heilman

I always reflect on *Offenbach Overtures* with a smile. I remember having such a good time during the creation process – the music is so engaging, and Paul really got us right into the "fast lane" with it, matching the intensity/density of the material so nicely to the score, and as a group we seemed quite good at working out the details as we went. I especially recall us all laughing a lot when we started making the Duel section, as (again) the music seemed to beg for such silliness. Partnering in that part with Andrew Asnes was great fun, and, directly after that, I so used to love looking into Caryn Heilman's eyes during the romantic barcarolle.

– Thomas Patrick

James Samson, Annmaria Mazzini and cast members

*"Taylor-ed to keep you in stitches."*
– Terry Teachout, *New York Daily News*

# EVENTIDE

The premise of the dance was to see what emotions can be conjured from simple walking patterns. When Paul created the duet for Andrew Asnes and me – our first together – we felt we weren't "dancing" enough, that nothing was happening. It felt so stark, so minimal. We were barely sweating, and slightly disappointed as a result. It was an uncomfortable and vulnerable place for a performer. Not until we saw all the duets strung together side by side did we realize the importance of what the three of us were making together. Our duet is part of a romantic fairy-tale and for me, a fiercely personal one. Paul couldn't have known that Andrew and I would, briefly, become a couple. Was it life imitating art? Paul is a master at giving poignancy to things we already know to be true – in this case, that people fall in love, and often they move on.

– Rachel Berman

I was a rookie in '96 when Paul made *Eventide*; that was my first experience with his genius. I came from a sports background – my dream was to be the shortstop for the New York Yankees – so physical dances fit me well. *Eventide* was a lot of walking and partnering but it was one of my favorite dances; I felt I could just perform as myself. That last section is amazingly designed. Walking with my partner to the Vaughan Williams music, those phrases touched my heart; the idea that you fall in love but always say goodbye at the end. *Eventide* is so simple and effortless, but it touches audiences deeply, and even touches the dancers performing the work. I'm very grateful to have been part of Paul's work, both as a dancer and as an observer of his process. It helps my choreography now; something about taking your time. Sometimes simple is best.

– Takehiro Ueyama

James Samson, Laura Halzack, Francisco Graciano and Heather McGinley

*"The American spirit soars when Taylor's dances and dancers meet, but rarely has it reached the sublime heights of this piece."*

– Octavio Roca, *San Francisco Chronicle*

# PIAZZOLLA CALDERA

Day one of *Piazzolla Caldera,* the usual nervous excitement was magnified by the arrival of a film crew making what would become an Oscar-nominated documentary. With cameras rolling, Paul and I began the intimate process of setting the choreography in a sort of conversational way. I assumed that working with me was like pulling teeth for Paul, yet he was at ease, patient and giving. His creative ideas were flowing in the opening scene's placement of men pitted against women; the aggressive, fiery duet between Lisa and Patrick; the narcissistic, cold love between Silvia and Andrew that was so beautiful it hurt; and the inventive, drunken, ambivalent movement of Tom's and Richard's duet. My memories are intensity, confidence, creativity and camaraderie. I felt the comfort of home, a sense of belonging, appreciated, respected and challenged. It was thrilling to be surrounded by such great talent and artistry. There's such joy in working your hardest.

– Francie Huber Mourad

It was really special to be a part of this dance. When we heard Gidon Kremer playing that gorgeous music we knew it was going to be great. I found Paul's impulse to make a dance involving this gritty and violent kind of love very interesting, especially so because it would be only his dance vocabulary and not that of actual tango that we'd be using. From the start the movement felt so right and married so well to the music. I was honored to be featured in a duet (with the incredibly-strong Richard Chen See) in the "Celos." And as if any more inspiration was needed it was tremendous to begin the dance facing those beautiful ladies across the stage. I'm so very glad that the making of this dance was captured in the film "Dancemaker"…it was a great experience to be a part of.

– Thomas Patrick

Parisa Khobdeh, Robert Kleinendorst and Annmaria Mazzini

*"Seethes and flares with sexuality and…develops a huge erotic charge."*
– Clement Crisp, *Financial Times of London*

# THE WORD

Paul started by working just with me on a 90-second solo. It was the first time I ever worked with him one-on-one. He had me doing all this knee work that I wasn't prepared for. Blood everywhere – my knees bled through my sweatpants. I could have bled to death and I wouldn't have cared, I was so excited. But after a while Paul asked, "You want to go get some kneepads?" I walked into the second studio and everybody's jaw dropped from fear when they saw my blood-stained sweats. Then I asked if anybody had kneepads, and they cracked up. At the end of the day Paul said, "I think I want it all to be from the other side – can you reverse the entire thing?" In the storyline, my movement imitates Lisa Viola's, so he actually developed some of her movement on me first.

– Andrew LeBeau

Paul has a gift for exploring the many aspects of humanity, from the most sublime, ethereal spirits to the ugliest part of us. I was never sure what we were in *The Word*: innocent schoolboys whipped into subservience by that green lizard-girl, or willing participants in a twisted army, ready to stamp out anyone who wasn't "one of us." It was almost scary how you'd get caught up in the mob mentality, finding satisfaction in the rhythm of our movement, feeling fiercer as the dance progressed. If I could see the audience well enough, I'd pick out one person to stare down during certain sections of the dance and try to make them sweat. I have the greatest respect and a heart full of love and admiration for Paul. Thanks for letting me dance your dances – the best ever, in my book. I loved the ugly ones as much as, if not more than, the pretty ones.

– Kristi Egtvedt Somers

Laura Halzack, Eran Bugge and Aileen Roehl

*"Taylor's comment on the crushing impact of religious conformity."*
– Wilma Salisbury, *Cleveland Plain Dealer*

# CASCADE

Paul's creation of *Cascade* is one of my fondest memories as a dancer. In the duet, I had the great pleasure of working with Patrick Corbin as Paul slowly unfurled it upon us. He guided us through our use of the subtle, which is at the heart of this duet. Dancing it felt similar to a life partner sensing what you need without asking, by simply knowing. Moving with Patrick was like sharing a wave with him. The choreography is simply luscious. It was a true gift Paul gave to us. A beautiful example of less is more. Recently, Patrick and I were teaching together in the Taylor Summer Intensive at the University of Michigan, where we set the duet on the students there. It was like riding a bike: one never forgets.

– Maureen Mansfield Kaddar

*Cascade*, like many of Paul's works, presents the dancers with multiple challenges. Stay in formation with the other dancers, jump faster than you think you can, balance off-kilter, turn in an awkward way and make it all look like it is the easiest and most graceful thing you could possibly be doing. When we made the dance back in the late '90s (fun to say that), Paul created a little brotherhood of men in the quintet that starts the dance. The steps were fast and awkward and it was not easy. I mean it's hard to jump backwards, reaching up with curved arms, arching your back with double attitude shapes with both legs, while trying to stay in formation and trying not to hit the women passing between us. I remember Francie Huber told me that for her solo, Paul brought in a Hula book as inspiration for shapes and movements.

– Andrew Asnes

Jamie Rae Walker, Laura Halzack, Michelle Fleet and Parisa Khobdeh

*"One of Mr. Taylor's most elegant pure-dance works."*
– Anna Kisselgoff, *New York Times*

# ARABESQUE

I was thrilled that Paul would choreograph a solo for me in *Arabesque*; for the first time, I would be alone onstage performing a section Paul created on me. But I was nervous, too. In the past, I had the help of my fellow dancers to remember sequences choreographed on the spot, but this would be my first time alone in the studio with Paul! I was very happy to see Amy Young in the room on the first day of rehearsals; she was to understudy, and with her help I felt more secure during the creation of the solo. The music was an eerie flute melody by Debussy; Paul wanted me to move like an animal in a forest, a mysterious being with dark powers. At one point he asked if I could get up from the floor with straight legs from my wide open leg split. I said I didn't have Lisa Viola's hips. We laughed and he let me bend both legs and power myself upright in a wide fourth position. Thank God.

– Silvia Nevjinsky

During that rehearsal period we had a huge rainstorm and the Seventh Avenue subway line was flooded. Takehiro and I both lived on the Upper West Side; we met and tried to get on a bus but they were all jam-packed so we walked to 42nd Street and took the "R" train to the studio, arriving 90 minutes late. To my surprise, Paul had decided to choreograph a solo on me that day! Instead he choreographed it on Patrick, who taught it to me in about ten minutes. Without any warm-up and with my legs a wreck from walking so much, I had to dance it in front of Paul and hope I wouldn't lose the solo. I was super-psyched that Paul wanted to make a solo on me, and devastated that it didn't happen. Patrick was a terrific turner; thank goodness he didn't throw in a bunch of turns. I always wondered if it would have been any different had it been set on me.

– Andrew LeBeau

Heather McGinley and Michael Novak

*"Fierce, impossibly swift dancing that blends earthy ferocity with skimming airiness."*
– Susan Reiter, *Newsday*

# BLACK TUESDAY

When Paul told us he was using songs from the Great Depression I was thrilled because I was a big fan of the sassy characters in '30s movies. When he played "The Boulevard of Broken Dreams" for me I knew it was going to be something special. "You're going to be a streetwalker," he said, "you know what that means, right?" Immediately we connected with the injustice of this girl's sad situation. As a bonus, Susan McGuire was assisting in the process, and the memory of the sultry, tragic heroine she evoked so movingly in *Last Look* influenced us as we found earthy, languid material to mix with the fiery anger. Despite the heaviness of the subject matter, we still had fun and laughed as we worked. I always found that to be one of the most curious and endearing surprises of working with Paul! That solo was such a gift, it's an experience I will always treasure.

– Annmaria Mazzini

Paul asked me to watch Christopher Walken in "Pennies From Heaven" to prepare for the role of the pimp. We worked on steps and Paul offered notes like, "Be more slimy" or "Something's always wiggling." He spent most of his time working on things for the women, and would ask me: "What will you do after they do that?" and I'd be ready with something we made earlier – it was very organic. When he asked me to strut in front of them, I thought it'd be funny to do a low walk and Paul said, "Lower." When my knees were a hair's breadth from the ground, he laughed. I loved that he challenged us so a piece of our DNA could merge with the dance. And the cigar – I spent a lot of time thinking about when to dangle it, when to bounce it, and when to point it upwards. In this case, a cigar was more than a cigar, and we all knew it.

– Orion Duckstein

Annmaria Mazzini, Kristi Egtvedt, Lisa Viola, Maureen Mansfield, Julie Tice and Amy Young

*"No other choreographer… has given us such a picture of the way we were in 20th-Century America."*
– Jean Battey Lewis, *Washington Times*

# PROMETHEAN FIRE

*Promethean* flowed out of Paul. It's as if he were in direct contact with something greater. We finished half of the duet and then I threw my back out. I missed a few days of work and Michael Trusnovec completed the duet. The switch came when Lisa and I have a confrontational "conversation." The first time I saw Lisa fly through the air at Michael I gasped; then I was filled with dread when I realized that would be me. It was a bittersweet moment because I knew I was passing the mantle to Michael – my years as a Taylor dancer were coming to an end. People say *Promethean* is Paul's response to 9/11. For me it was about Stephanie Reinhart. Stephanie was dying, leaving Charlie and Ariane behind. I really loved Stephanie. *Promethean* will always be for Charlie, Ariane and Stephanie. Every time I danced it, it was for them.

– Patrick Corbin

Paul chose to use the entire company of 16 dancers for this latest work. Unheard of, since there are always understudies left out to cover parts. It felt like just what we needed. With the timing of its creation, *Promethean Fire* became what most say is a comment to what occurred on 9/11. I remember Paul saying the work was just about passion. I think it's about trust. Trusting that you are in good hands, which we have with Paul. Trust in your colleagues, that we are there for each other. Paul's trust in us. And trusting that under any circumstances, the human spirit, in time, can rise above it all. I loved being a part of *Promethean Fire*. I'm lucky to say I never missed a performance. Though something I did miss: getting to my partner. On the catch. Twice.

– Lisa Viola

Michael Trusnovec and Parisa Khobdeh

*"It has grandeur, majesty and a spiritual dimension."*
– Anna Kisselgoff, *New York Times*

# DANTE VARIATIONS

Working on *Dante Variations* was a great experience. I've always loved Paul's darker works. The first section seemed to have poured out of our bodies that day in the studio. I can only imagine it was the imagery of the tortured souls in Dante's *Inferno*. How Paul exposed these tortured souls and bodies left me feeling sad, exhausted, hopeless and sometimes laughing. I particularly remember feeling frightened when I found out I was to be blindfolded on stage and had to dance the remainder of my solo this way. This fear enabled me to play with many ideas about the dance and myself. It also forced me to build more trust for my dance partners who guided me gently to safety when it was over.

– Michelle Fleet

Starting work on *Dante Variations*, I was thrilled when Paul told us he wanted to make a dance delving into the dark imagery of Dante's *Inferno* – the twisted, tortured souls damned to Hell seemed the perfect inspiration for a Taylor dance. He turned the idea into a satisfying, raw, muscular, flailing, gnarled, sensual dance propelled by the creepy Ligeti organ score. I honestly didn't think I could move as fast as Paul asked me to in the short solo he created for me – one of the most choreographically dense minutes of dancing of my career thus far.

– Michael Trusnovec

Lisa Viola, Robert Kleinendorst, Annmaria Mazzini and Michael Trusnovec

*"Tales of violence, lasciviousness and death...*
*left one feeling amused, hurt, emotionally drained."*
– Paul Horsley, *Kansas City Star*

# BANQUET OF VULTURES

From the premiere to the season's final performance, *Banquet* sparked a feverish response from audiences across the country. The sinister world Paul created intrigued people and enabled them to viscerally experience and kinesthetically feel the gravity of the political situation at the time. It was created during a time of war and was relevant to so many generations, as so much of Paul's work is. While I was never concerned how the audience would react after the curtain came down, it never ceased to amaze me how they vehemently roared in response to the world Paul created on stage. I had to prepare mentally as much as physically to commit to the character Paul created. It challenged me artistically, and was significantly darker than any role I danced previously. Paul gave me the freedom to explore the depth of the role under his guidance and instruction. It was a gift that I am forever grateful for.

– Julie Tice

Paul told me I'd have a solo with repeated falls, so I worked on those. My initial impulse was to fall, get up, travel and fall again, but he wanted me to fall and rise in one place, and fall on every different body part I could. He took my movements and changed some directions, some spacing, and the order; the cool part was playing off each other's ideas. He wanted me to make noises and grab my chest as if I were being possessed, so throughout the solo I gasp and claw at my chest. That last jump he made bigger and bigger and bigger until it became a giant windmill jump landing flat on my side – painful! After I go limp I stand up like a ragdoll as though the possessor is learning to use my body. Finally I move to center stage and become in complete control of my movements. The possession is complete.

– Robert Kleinendorst

Michael Trusnovec and Julie Tice

*"Taylor might be the only American choreographer I would trust with the subject of war…."*
– Paul Horsley, *Kansas City Star*

# TROILUS AND CRESSIDA (REDUCED)

I can't help but remember creating *Troilus and Cressida (reduced)* in the old studio on Broadway; I sometimes miss its charm. This is one of Paul's short dances yet it packs quite a punch. I was one of the Greek warriors and was excited to learn that the dance was to be a comedy. Paul is great at creating funny and exaggerated movement, and I enjoyed the freedom he allowed us to develop our characters. One important aspect of the dance was the costumes. The three Greeks were to have capes, so in rehearsal we made sure to have long towels pinned around our necks to practice with. Nothing compared, however, to the real thing. As if the dance weren't funny enough, the costumes were sure to make it a comic masterpiece. Stitched padding made to look like six-pack abs, red crushed velvet tights, shoulder epaulets, an elaborate crown…and, oh yes, the long gold-adorned capes.

– James Samson

First, Paul called the four ladies into the studio, and then Bettie called me in. *I'm finally going to be the Romantic Male Lead!* Then Paul said, "You're going to be a dumb hobo," and that turned into Troilus. The character developed organically, including puffing out his cheeks to indicate utter confusion. As I began to fine tune I was always thinking, *What would Troilus do?* Lisa and I worked well together – we knew when to be the straight man and let the other person take the comedic lead. By the time we premiered the dance, we'd lost a sense of how funny it is, but the audience went insane… they literally screamed. Paul's comedic works have to be the cleanest, most precise, most well-rehearsed of his dances; more than any other genre, they're pretty perfect, and they only work if they're done the way he made them. Like a Swiss watch; no wasted movement.

– Robert Kleinendorst

Sean Mahoney, Jeffrey Smith and James Samson

*"Bright-spirited, belly-laugh humor."*
– Susan Broili, *Durham Herald-Sun*

# LINES OF LOSS

*Lines of Loss* was made near the end my career with the Company. Not wanting to leave yet, but knowing that it was probably time, was on my mind. Paul could probably sense this. He just can. This was the last solo Paul made on me. And having my friend and colleague Michael Trusnovec as my partner for the final duet made for a perfect closure to my time in the Company in so many ways. The vignettes throughout *Lines of Loss* could be glimpses into our own personal journeys. Struggling, attaining it, having it slip away. Friends made, some lost. Once young, now old. Good days and bad. Before you know it, the ride is over. Time flies when you do what you love and love what you do. Saying goodbye is hard. Letting go, even harder.

– Lisa Viola

Quiet rage, acceptance and peace of mind filled me when we danced *Lines of Loss*. It's a gift to be given the chance to visit a multitude of emotions each time we step on stage.

– Michelle Fleet

The first image Paul gave us was a newspaper photo of a soldier at a funeral: solemn, staunchly upright posture, chin lifted but eyes downcast; strong and composed but still projecting deep, contained emotions. *Lines* is a sad piece but still deeply satisfying to dance. I got to do the solo that came later in the dance, when the mad grief was finally released, what Paul titled "Loss of Composure." But my favorite memory of the dance was sitting backstage at the edge of the fourth wing to watch Lisa and Michael's heartbreaking duet. It was one of those extended moments in time I never wanted to miss.

– Annmaria Mazzini

Michael Trusnovec and Lisa Viola

*"Impossible to watch and not be moved to mourning."*
– Rachel Howard, *San Francisco Chronicle*

# DE SUEÑOS (OF DREAMS)

It was just after my two-year anniversary, and from day one, this creative process was different. Mr. Taylor was departing from expansive athleticism, and demanding precise focus, specificity of character, and subtlety of gesture. Having performed diverse Taylor dances from *Esplanade* to *Dust*, it was hard to put the explosive and grounded Taylor style on the shelf. Mr. Taylor coached me in taunting Rob's transvestite, to take my time and treat each gesture like a phrase in a conversation, paying close attention to focus, stance, and inclination of the body. This was the first time I understood the communicative power and extreme attention to detail in choreographing gesture. As a keen watcher of people, Mr. Taylor has mastered the skill of authentic human gesture while avoiding dramatic and mime-like caricature. In subsequent dances such as *Beloved Renegade*, he has continued to make statements about the human condition using gesture.

– Jeffrey Smith

*De Sueños* was the second dance that Paul created after I joined the Company. At first, it appeared that I was not cast in the work. Then, unexpectedly, the second week of rehearsal I was called into the studio. I was surprised, thrilled, and terribly nervous. Paul asked me to do a long, slow series of *bourrées* across the floor, and so began one of the most challenging and wondrous moments of my career. He had me try everything that day: long, slow balances, difficult contortions, and even a bit of acrobatics. All of this was incredibly difficult while attempting to project cosmic serenity, but it was a dream, and I loved every moment of it! That day Paul showed me that I could push myself beyond what I believed were the boundaries of my physical potential, but more importantly he stretched my mind and introduced me to the universe of artistic possibility.

– Laura Halzack

Laura Halzack and Michael Trusnovec

*"Thank goodness, Taylor's [dreams] are more thrilling than mine."*
– Susan Broili, *Durham Herald-Sun*

# BELOVED RENEGADE

There was a glint in Paul's eye when he asked if I'd read "Leaves of Grass." I bought a copy and was swept up by its pace, colors, emotion and gravity. I could feel it was special for Paul; the dance seemed to be coming from a deep, personal place. It's the only choreographic experience I've had where he was visibly moved on several occasions. There was also a magic between Laura and me. The minimal choreography helped amplify the tender, wordless conversation happening between us. When Patrick Corbin came to me in tears after the premiere, calling it a masterpiece, I was utterly confused. How did I not know this? Strange, when you're in a work, how difficult it is to sense if it's powerful. Audiences have had forceful responses to my character: "You're Walt Whitman." "You're Paul Taylor." I've always thought of my role as "everyman" – one blade of grass in an infinite field of green.

– Michael Trusnovec

The studio took on the aura of another world when Paul began *Beloved Renegade*. Watching him create a transcendent place where negative space and subtle gesture were as grand as anything virtuosic was to observe a master at work. I'll never forget the sensation that something magical was transpiring. Out of this dance came one of my most cherished characters – the Dark Angel – and the beginning of a dear relationship with my dance partner and friend, Michael Trusnovec. "I need you to be cool, but sweet," Paul said. This opened my imagination and enabled me to go in search of this gentle "deliveress" – a gift and a journey I cherish every time I perform *Renegade*. Concerning Michael, you learn a lot about somebody when you have to stare into their eyes for a long time without giggling. I'll forever be humbled and grateful for being a part of this masterpiece, and I don't think I'll ever tire of performing it.

– Laura Halzack

Laura Halzack and Michael Trusnovec

*"A work of philosophic as well as dramatic power."*
– Alastair Macaulay, *New York Times*

# ALSO PLAYING

Dancing *Also Playing* feels like what I imagine being in a Vaudeville show would have been like. Never in one dance have I had so many costume and accessory changes – and all of them bordering on unachievable speed. Paul made it very clear that good comedy required us to play it perfectly straight. He created my role of an overly confident and, as it turned out, accident-prone ballerina. At the premiere, to my shock and horror, in the first duet my huge ballroom skirt suddenly dropped to my ankles and I had to improvise through what felt like an eternity with many failed attempts to keep it on. As with other mishaps in *Also Playing*, Paul decided he liked it and insisted that it stay in the dance just as it had happened. The trick was then to replicate in each performance what had been purely accidental. It's probably the closest to Vaudeville I'll ever get.

– Jamie Rae Walker

You have to stay true to your character and your relationship to the people around you. I come on stage for a tarantella flanked by two guys. Paul wanted me to slap my thigh with a tambourine, then slap my butt, then slap the boys. On the first day, I broke right through the tambourine. My thighs were black and blue, and the boys were black and blue as well because I hit them with as much fervor as I hit myself. Paul emphasized the character's absolute belief in what she's doing; ultimately that's what's funny. Julie danced the Dying Swan to the hilt. Since she had short hair, Santo made her crown with a long bun attached. In the tech rehearsal for the premiere, the crown fell off, so she grabbed it and put it back on *with authority* – backwards. But she never came out of character, and that became a great part of the dance.

– Parisa Khobdeh

Julie Tice, Michelle Fleet, Annmaria Mazzini and Michael Apuzzo

*"Belongs to that rich genre in which theater is about theater itself."*
– Alastair Macaulay, *New York Times*

# BRIEF ENCOUNTERS

*Brief Encounters* was one of the first dances Paul created on me. On day one he called the Company into the rehearsal room, lit a cigarette and said "Back to work." I was in the first section he made. He let us try new solo jumps and lifts with our partners; it felt very comfortable to explore movement with him as he created the piece. A week later, he pulled me out of Company class and into the hallway, where costume designer Santo Loquasto held the smallest underwear I'd ever seen. Paul said, "Puzzo, try on your new costume." It was me, a dance belt, a homemade pair of briefs – a pun on the dance's title – and two artistic geniuses. Paul squinted at me in the costume and muttered, "A lot of skin, huh?" Blushing, I *really* wanted to get back to work. It was the "briefest" costume fitting of my career.

– Michael Apuzzo

This is a very sexual dance. When Paul made the duet in the last section, he wanted Sean and me to dance through it very slowly and with lots of tension. I think he wanted the virility and discomfort of two heterosexual men writhing around each other to be conveyed unintentionally. Maybe it was. In the last section the whole cast begins on stage – the men upstage, the women downstage. Paul had each man go to the woman downstage of him but since there was an uneven number of people in the cast, I was alone. He stepped back and saw that everyone had a partner but me and said, "Oh well, I guess you don't have anyone. Well, that's okay. Sometimes that's just what happens." He started to walk away but looked back at me and said with a devilish smirk, "But not *you*. You're never left alone – I just know."

– Francisco Graciano

Michael Apuzzo, Francisco Graciano, James Samson, Jeffrey Smith and Sean Mahoney

*"Every emotion and meeting seems young, pristine, mysterious."*
– Alastair Macaulay, *New York Times*

# THREE DUBIOUS MEMORIES

While Paul was choreographing, a camera crew was capturing the process, and doing their best to film amid the dancers without getting a toe in the eye. Paul was on fire! He was rolling out the dance phrases and it was all I could do to keep up. At the end of one of the rehearsal days, I jokingly asked if I could see the film footage just so I could make sure I remembered all the steps. Besides needing to have every ounce of "grey matter" working to the best of its ability, I also had to call upon some emotional demons. This was the first time in my dance career that I was asked to portray a dark, sinister character. Not easy. I did my best. And I choose to remember it as the dance that helped me widen my spectrum of ability.

– Sean Mahoney

It's an honor to originate any role in one of Paul's creations, and who wouldn't want to be The Woman in Red? On the third day, he choreographed a duet for Rob and me – our first and only love duet in all the 12 years we had been working together. Sean entered next as an aggressor and we were more than ready to help create some violent movement. We love to be that physical. Each progressive scene had a different style, which I began to see was a unique manner in which Paul chose to tell this story. In our third scenario, I became the aggressor and at the premiere performance in Richardson, Texas, a woman yelled out, "You go girl!" She obviously identified with my character. I particularly enjoyed the day he choreographed my character's final statement. Without hesitation he gave me clear, strong yet desperate movements to work with. It was a truly memorable experience.

– Amy Young

Amy Young and cast members

*"Searching for beauty and significance
in even the tawdriest aspects of the human condition."*
– Robert Johnson, *Star Ledger*

# GOSSAMER GALLANTS

I learned a really important lesson when Paul began choreographing *Gossamer Gallants*. The movement was specific and fast, and, being relatively new, I wanted to impress the boss. Naturally, I approached the dance very seriously. And then I went to my costume fitting. There I stood, in front of the amazing Santo Loquasto, in a giant bug muscle-suit – wings and all. As I was looking at myself in the mirror, I realized that my approach to the dance may have been a tad hyper-serious. The moral: never underestimate a costume's power to inform your portrayal of a character – especially a comedic one. *Gossamer* taught me to appreciate the value of a good laugh. In fact, if there's one thing I have really grown to love about the Company it's our ability to have fun with each other on stage.

– Michael Novak

All through the creative period, it seemed Paul knew that what we were doing was silly, and I think he got a kick out of our antics. It flowed easily and we all had a good time making it. The day he made the women's section, Michelle was wearing giant earrings and I think that's partly why he has her shimmy her shoulders over and over. He liked the way the earrings shook so much that he asked Santo for earrings to be built into our headpieces. The first time we showed *Gossamer* during a private rehearsal, the ladies in the audience were thrilled with how the lady bugs triumphed over the men. Performing *Gossamer* for a receptive audience enables us to take it to the next level of silliness; almost every time, we have them laughing from the men's very first entrance. When the audience is with us we totally feed off that energy and ham it up even more.

– Eran Bugge

Francisco Graciano and Michael Apuzzo

*"A sex comedy… Taylor's bugs are dead funny."*
– Robert Gottlieb, *New York Observer*

# TO MAKE CROPS GROW

My first encounter with Paul Taylor and his work was at South-ern Methodist University auditioning for *Esplanade*. I remem-ber almost walking out because I didn't understand the point of walking, skipping, sliding – that's not dance! But I stayed and Paul's work changed my entire life. My perspective as an artist, my imagination of what dance could be, and even my career path changed.  As a "new" dancer, it's been a pleasure getting acquainted with Paul artistically in *To Make Crops Grow* and *American Dreamer*.  He continues to amaze, with a vision far beyond what is immediately evident to me as an individual. It's been a joy to watch both of these new dances blossom as they become fully realized, and to enjoy audience reaction. This experience has been insightful when we, as artist-detectives, delve into the past to recreate the passion and beauty of this incredible catalog.

– George Smallwood

This was one dance where we knew going in how it would end – I'd read "The Lottery" in my American high school in Germany – but we didn't know how Paul would get us there. It's interesting to play a child: finding a child's posture and short attention span, and not fully understanding what's going on. We made up a story that Parisa is my stepmom and not happy about it; perhaps she's from elsewhere and mar-ried Michael not knowing he had a child. Paul was specific about my having pigtails with bows; I put one bow in my hair in rehearsals so Cisco would have something to pull. Paul always said, "You're going to have *two* bows" – his attention to detail is unwavering. This is a gestural, character-driven dance. My childhood ballet teachers always stressed acting and working on character, so Paul's gestural dances aren't too far out of my comfort zone.

– Aileen Roehl

Parisa Khobdeh and cast members

# PERPETUAL DAWN

Playful and lighthearted, *Perpetual Dawn* is an uplifting dance to perform. On day one, Paul said it would be a portrait of young love. We are often paired off, although more than once a dancer is left searching for a companion. In a duet with Michael Apuzzo, he and I swirl around each other to the floor. I then run away, only to be whisked off my feet and over his head. Just after, in a very different duet, Amy Young and I have a detailed conversation of gestures. Paul let us in on some of his intended narrative, but we were left to imagine our own secret dialogue.

– Heather McGinley

As always, Paul gave us a little taste of the music before he began. Light and airy, the music enabled us to "feel" his brainstorms. He wanted gentle love. He wanted calm connections. He also wanted energetic relationships. With the use of these mental springboards, we were able to launch ourselves into the air. Duets, solos, group sections: I knew exactly what they meant. It was a beautifully soft piece with sparks of energetic romance. Time to take it to the theater. The first time I saw the backdrop, everything changed. Santo Loquasto's use of muted ambers, reds, browns, and yellows took me to a completely different place. I realized that the relationships within *Perpetual Dawn* weren't simple. They were as complex as his use of colors in the sky at dawn. It forced me to dig deeper into my dancing. Not to take it for granted. Paul's springboards gave me my dance narrative. Santo's backdrop showed me that Paul's ideas run quite deep.

– Sean Mahoney

Francisco Graciano and Eran Bugge

*"Made me totally happy:*
*Young people frolicking, chasing each other in innocent attraction."*
– Robert Gottlieb, *New York Observer*

Bettie de Jong and Paul Taylor in *Public Domain*

# "MY SWEET DANCERS..."  (1974)

Here's a letter for you. We could chat instead but it is important to get these words just right and I do not trust my adlib. The topic is an amorphous one and, in an attempt to be clear, I may say the same things several times with different words. Or in the same words. You know we all hear and see those things we prefer to and this way you may cross out the wordings you do not care for and still have at least one version left that you may like to perhaps read over and over. Please keep this tucked in each of your costumes where it will be handy to get at.

It is a topic that makes me a little shy to keep mentioning out loud though it has to do with our work. It is, in a way, personal and maybe better left that way. It is something that has been on my mind for a while now and, though I have brought it up before, I feel I did not express it fully or strongly enough at our rehearsal times, which is where it properly belongs. Please understand that dissatisfaction with you has not prompted me. Far from it. You are all dancing so well and with such security that I think you might like an additional challenge. There should be always one more mountain and it would be unhealthy if we thought we had ever reached our peak. Taking a good questioning look at ourselves may be an uncomfortable effort, but it can be a valuable one. If you think I am being critical of you, know that this grows out of questions I ask myself about my own dancing. It is also from performances I see you give. Or, I should say, parts of performances. You know I am not out front and my eyes aren't peeled in the wings all the time. Nevertheless, I still soak up a certain amount of your doings onstage, enough that I can tell there is an area that each of us can enlarge in. It is something called zunch. I think we can dance with more of it. Or at least more consistently with what we have. I want you to have no doubts about its importance to dance and dance audiences. Zunch is a word that is not in any dictionary. In Spain they call it *duende*. It is related to full generosity or passion.

I have seen zunchistic dancing in each of you at some time or other or else there would be no use to bring it up for it can't be taught. It is something you all have the capacity for and entered the Company with. We all know we are each strong willed and underneath have something that goes with individualism: grade AA egos. Your sweetness and care for us as a troupe keeps you working together more or less smoothly but, compliant as you may choose to be, we know you are not in this unlikely occupation to do self-sacrificing genuflections. And I am glad. (Though I must admit there have been times I wished the guy you call big cheese had been buttered up more.) I am suggesting we take these dangerous nuclear egos and use them for all the benefit they are worth. They are a resource if they can produce zunchionate dancing.

Please do not get what I mean mixed up with hamming, bad taste or strain. Those qualities are the result of falseness or inappropriateness, not zunch. And zunch does not mean being especially erotic, though people don't mind that, of course, if you are truly and appropriately erotic. Some people say eroticism is what dance is all about.

Zunch is the thing – here we go, at last – that sets the exciting dancer apart from the adequate one. You've heard someone say, "She is a lovely dancer." Well, gals, is that your idea of the ultimate in compliments? I doubt it. You are there to rivet, not be only lovely. Is "very fine" enough for us gents? It may do very well, depending on who says it and how, but surely, shouldn't we transfix? Zunch is the difference, you bet. It is the magic that sticks with the watchers after we are done. Not the review or the film or the von Laban notation. It is the ability to focus what may be only an infinitesimal gesture and hurl it *splatch* from one soul to another. It can be the little extra push that may make a leap only an eighth of an inch higher but astonishes with its valor because it comes from the dancer's total commitment. It is whatever your favorite dancers do to allow you to see their special and mysterious human values.

It is not really a partly open mouth, burning eyes, spread fingers and forward-tilted pelvis. But if we did this position with true conviction it might pass, I suppose. Zunch is nothing we can clamp onto the outside of our bodies and hold there no matter what. It is something that has to ebb and flow and breathe. There is no single key to every door, no one energy for every step. It is sometimes as simple as the difference between looking towards another dancer onstage, or really seeing that person. But if really seeing makes us late, let's not do it.

It is the difference between us going to the theater and earning our salaries or going to the theater and putting that audience in debt to us.

Zunch is fullness. It is not merely authority and, naturally, not technical brilliance. We cannot do much without authority and technique, but zunch should underlie these other talents – and not take a back seat to them. Perhaps we tend to wall up zunch in our concern with other qualities we wish to excel in. Or hide behind, perhaps? Sad thought. Zunch is being generous with your spirit. As differentiated from that thing in us that is not body, brain or cute personality.

Zunch is opening up. Focusing intent in or out. Turning the burner on. Going beyond. Isn't it what makes a dancer out of a pedestrian? Both walk, sure, but one is illuminating, the other locomoting.

Zunchistic dancing needs no special choreography. Any step can get the zunch treatment. We can do the *Epitaphs* slump with zunchionate lack of energy. Or throw away a step with zunchy off-handedness. Or stumble, glide, twitch, float, mince or be stock still with it. Some of our dances demand a cool and unspecific zunch. Whatever step we perform remains dull rote until it is brought to life. Are we to show the public an assortment of choreographic moves or are we to show them dance? Ourselves dancing. Do not misunderstand – zunch does not require us to shout ME ME or for us to act a role, necessarily. It is more the gathering of our intents and instincts and letting them out from inside. Our instincts will help us know what is right. Do not mistrust them. They are close knit to all of this. However, if my instinct disagrees with yours, you will hear a loud "Stop that, you are ruining my dance!"

Just how far can we go as dancers? I do not think we want to settle on a comfortable limit. When we perform are our pores and nerve ends awake to the light? Can we hear a stagehand's cigar ash drop to the floor? Let's hope not, the smelly things. No need to turn to see what just happened behind us. We just know. Why not? If we suffer a cut while in view, perhaps we can even postpone bleeding; with the will, the senses, and our bodies all wound together these extreme things could be not only possible but natural.

The boards of the stage or where the legs are hung don't define the limits of the space we are in. *We* do. We can enter and bring our space with us. We can be at the vanishing point on a horizon or we can be within a small contained space. A tiny turtle. The best proportioned and equipped stage in the world does not make it a special place. The dancer does – by starting a circuit flowing, a kind of St. Elmo's fire that radiates around the dancer, the defined space and the audience. Not technique, physical beauty, choreography or anything short of zunch will click on this circuit. Let's try to remember this next time we get a postage-stamp stage with inadequate lights. It may not solve the problem but it won't hurt to be hopeful.

Besides making an illusion of space, we can even give an illusion to our bodies. Unfortunately, zunch can't completely hide overweight. But we can direct the public's eye to where we want it. Torsos or legs or necks can seem longer. Arms don't have to stop at the fingertips. We can lengthen, if we will, into the next county. Why do certain dancers seem so tall? No, Carolyn [Adams], not because they get cast with shorter dancers. Well, the point is not that I want us to start changing from size to size like Alice. That won't get us anywhere much. I mention this only as another of the endless possibilities that zunchy dancing can open up. Maybe it could even open up better bookings.

Dancing with zunch or full generosity is:
1) what zaps the viewers
2) being somebody – yourself only more so
3) taking ambition and ego and transforming them into something worth watching
4) possessing a face like a frog, no neck or chin at all, pancake feet and, in spite of it, enchanting the audience (more possible where general audiences still love the underdog more than his or her looks)
5) the Big Dare that could end up looking sublime if we make it, idiotic if we don't
6) being right or maybe even wrong but with a flourish that convinces
7) what my dog Elmer is full of when he gets let out
8) those damn little "flags of celebration," as Martha liked to say, "all over the bodah," which loses something in type. Maybe you might hear her say it out loud sometime
9) burning a candle to Pan, or Shiva, or whatever dance God you may invent
10) looking like we are putting ourselves out but not in a way that the public pities or worries about our well-being
11) what Eileen [Cropley] did that time in Israel when she wandered onto a rifle range and heard bullets whistling over her head. It was a little circling dance, as I remember, and she screamed eek! eek! eek! I remember onstage times too, Crops, love, but this one was unusual. Such fast footwork.
12) What Edwin Denby refers to when he wrote of Markova: "the rare grace of spirit which her dancing figure communicates." Thinking of it, you must read or re-read his *Looking at the Dance*. If you have no copy borrow mine.

So much for the definitions.

Is it so puzzling why some of our performances are more alive than others? What causes those special magic times? Is it strange that they happen sometimes when we are over-tired or injured or have lousy stages to cope with? It's puzzling that they do not necessarily happen when we are in ideal circumstances or are rested and happy. Or that sometimes when we think we have sinned unpardonably in our dancing, *that* is the very audience that responds so well. Perhaps it is desperation that gives us more adrenaline or makes us relax. Perhaps it happens at a premiere when we think the most we can do is remember our steps. What if we have to resort to enforced desperation to be able to give that little extra something! Unpleasant thought.

There must be some way to re-create those shining times and make them consistent. It is easy for us to say that Theater is a two-way street and the audience has to do their share. Okay, but we must assume it is us, not them, because we never really know it is the audience's fault, do we? Critics are another matter. One can get to know their individual brand of sensitivity by their writing and ignore the goony ones if we want. Audiences are harder to write off. Occasionally, they may seem goony, too, but we must assume that there is always at least one person among the others whose life we may enrich.

I had hoped this letter would inspire and uplift. Reading it over, I see that the tone came out not grand but informal and perhaps you have had a few chuckles instead of thrills and uplift. Maybe Lila [York] will be thinking, "*Now* he says he wants zunch. Oh well, I think I'll give it a whirl." Or Bettie [de Jong]: "Oh, that Paul! What does he think I have been doing all these years? He is so provocative!" (Dear Dutch Treat, never mind all this zunch talk, just try to remember *provocative* is good, *provoking* bad.) Although the aim is grand, it seems just as well the tone be casual. Let's not overdo our efforts to please. Let's just be ourselves – but more so.

– Paul Taylor

# COMPANY MEMBERS 1954–2014

Janet Aaron Nightingale
Geulah Abrahams
Carolyn Adams
Ruth Andrien
Michael Apuzzo
Toby Armour
Andrew Asnes
Pina Bausch
Heather Berest
Rachel Berman
Shareen Blair
Donald Boiteau
Joseph Bowie
Elizabeth Bragg
Karen Brooke Levey
Eran Bugge
Elie Chaib
Richard Chen See
Mary Cochran
Joan Coddington
Patrick Corbin
Hernando Cortez
Lorraine Crocket
Eileen Cropley
Therese Cura
Phena Darner
Charlene Davis
Bettie de Jong
Laura Dean
Michael Deane
Anita Dencks
Constance Dinapoli
Senta Driver
Orion Duckstein*
Jill Echo*
Kristi Egtvedt Somers*
Thomas Evert
Daniel Ezralow
Viola Farber
Donya Feuer
Gerald Fitzgerald
Michelle Fleet*
Christopher Gillis
Toby Glanternik
Francisco Graciano*
Alice Temkin Green
David Grenke
Nicholas Gunn
Laura Halzack
Caryn Heilman
Linda Hodes
Francie Huber Mourad
Barbara Janezic
Kate Johnson
Robert Kahn
Akiko Kanda

James Karr
Elizabeth Keen
Sandra Keery
Linda Kent
Cliff Keuter
Nathaniel Keuter
Parisa Khobdeh
Renée Kimball Wadleigh
Sharon Kinney
Robert Kleinendorst*
Jane Kosminsky
Raymond Kurshals
Andrew LeBeau*
Daniel Lewis
Christina Lynch Markham*
Sean Mahoney*
Maureen Mansfield Kaddar
Bonnie Mathis
Joao Mauricio
Annmaria Mazzini*
Cathy McCann
Heather McGinley
Susan McGuire
Molly Moore
Earnest Morgan
Monica Morris
Silvia Nevjinsky
Maggie Newman
Jack Nightingale
Michael Novak
David Parsons
Thomas Patrick
Terry Pexton
Paul Plumadore
Robert Powell
Gregory Reynolds
Denise Roberts Hurlin
Mabel Robinson
Manuel Rodriguez
Aileen Roehl
Carol Rubenstein
Alec Rubin
James Samson
Marian Sarach
Ruby Shang
George Smallwood
Jeffrey Smith*
Leslie Snow
Eileen Stanford
Cynthia Stone Arenillas
Sandra Stone
Britt Swanson Cryer
Edward Talton-Jackson
Paul Taylor
Twyla Tharp
Ted Thomas

Doris Thurston
Julie Tice*
Kristi Tornga
Kenneth Tosti
Michael Trusnovec*
Barbara Tucker
Matt Turney
Takehiro Ueyama
Victoria Uris
Angela Vaillancourt
David Vaughan
Lisa Viola
Jeff Wadlington
Dan Wagoner
Jamie Rae Walker*
Elizabeth Walton
James Waring
Daniel (Williams) Grossman
Barry Wizoreck
Karla Wolfangle
Raegan Wood
Douglas Wright
Lila York
Amy Young*

**Taylor 2 Members**:
Tim Acito
Dara Adler
Rei Akazawa
Alana Allende
Hank Bamberger
Robin Branch
Winston Dynamite Brown
John Byrne*
Nic Ceynowa
Alison Cook
Gail Cox
Susan Dodge*
Lee Duveneck
John Eirich
Joseph Gallerizzo
Vernon Gooden
Shanti Guirao
Madelyn Ho
Justin Kahan
Michael Kerns
Chad Levy
Amy Marshall
Leajato Robinson
Manuel Sanchez
Amanda Stevenson
Rebecca Vargus
Latra Wilson
Jared Wootan*

*danced in both companies

# DANCES BY PAUL TAYLOR

Listed in order of their world premieres
*Commissioned score

**1    JACK AND THE BEANSTALK**
Music by Hy Gubernick*
Set and costumes by
    Robert Rauschenberg
Lighting by Marc May
First performed May 30, 1954

**2    CIRCUS POLKA**
Music by Igor Stravinsky
Costumes by Robert Rauschenberg
Lighting by Marc May and John Robertson
First performed March 15, 1955

**3    LITTLE CIRCUS**
Music by Igor Stravinsky
Set and costumes by Robert Rauschenberg
Lighting by John Robertson
First performed June 6, 1955

**4    3 EPITAPHS**
Early New Orleans jazz
Costumes by Robert Rauschenberg
Lighting by George Tacet
First performed March 27, 1956

**5    THE LEAST FLYCATCHER**
Music and costumes by
    Robert Rauschenberg*
First performed May 6, 1956

**6    UNTITLED DUET**
Done in silence
Costumes by Robert Rauschenberg
First performed May 6, 1956

**7    TROPES**
Folk music
Costume by Robert Rauschenberg
First performed December 4, 1956

**8    OBERTURA REPUBLICANA**
Music by Carlos Chávez
Costumes by James Waring
First performed December 4, 1956

**9    THE TOWER**
Music by John Cooper*
Set by Robert Rauschenberg
Costumes by Jasper Johns
First performed in 1957

**SEVEN NEW DANCES**
Costumes by Robert Rauschenberg
Lighting by Tharon Musser
**10    EPIC**: telephone time signal
**11    EVENTS I**: wind sounds
**12    RESEMBLANCE**: John Cage*
**13    PANORAMA**: heartbeat sounds
**14    DUET**: John Cage*
**15    EVENTS II**: rain sounds
**16    OPPORTUNITY**: "noise"
First performed October 20, 1957

**17    MAY APPLE**
Performed in silence
Costumes by Robert Rauschenberg
First performed March 18, 1958

**18    REBUS**
Music by David Hollister*
Costumes by Robert Rauschenberg
First performed March 18, 1958

**19    IMAGES AND REFLECTIONS**
Music by Morton Feldman
Costumes and props by
    Robert Rauschenberg
Lighting by Tharon Musser
First performed December 20, 1958

**20    IMAGES AND REFLECTIONS**
Version for television first performed
    February 13, 1960

**21    MERIDIAN**
Music by Pierre Boulez
Costumes by Louise Thompson
First performed February 13, 1960

**22    OPTION**
Music by Richard Maxfield*
Costumes by Louise Thompson
First performed February 13, 1960

**23    MERIDIAN (rechoreographed)**
Music by Morton Feldman
Costumes by Alex Katz
First performed June 10, 1960

**24    TABLET**
Music by David Hollister*
Set and costumes by Ellsworth Kelly
First performed July 1, 1960

**25    THE WHITE SALAMANDER**
Music by Joop Stokkermans*
Costumes by Henk de Vries
First performed October 11, 1960

**26    FIBERS**
Music by Arnold Schoenberg
Set and costumes by Rouben Ter-Arutunian
First performed January 14, 1961

**27    INSECTS AND HEROES**
Music by John Herbert McDowell*
Set and costumes by Rouben Ter-Arutunian
Lighting by Louise Guthman
First performed August 18, 1961

**28    JUNCTION**
Music by Johann Sebastian Bach
Set and costumes by Alex Katz
Lighting by William Ritman
First performed November 24, 1961

**29    TRACER**
Music by James Tenny*
Set piece and costumes by
    Robert Rauschenberg
First performed April 11, 1962

**30    AUREOLE**
Music by George Frideric Handel
Costumes by George Tacet
Lighting by Thomas Skelton
First performed August 4, 1962

**31    PIECE PERIOD**
Music by Vivaldi, Telemann, Haydn, Scarlatti,
    Beethoven and Bonporti
Costumes by John Rawlings
Lighting by Thomas Skelton
First performed November 8, 1962

**32    LA NEGRA**
Mariachi music
Costumes and lighting by George Tacet
First performed January 24, 1963

**33    FIBERS**
Duet version for television first aired
    May 20, 1963

**34    SCUDORAMA**
Music by Clarence Jackson*
Set and costumes by Alex Katz
Lighting by Thomas Skelton
First performed August 10, 1963

**35    POETRY IN MOTION**
Music by Leopold Mozart
Co-choreographed with Katherine Litz
Costumes by Katherine Litz and
    George Tacet
Lighting by Thomas Skelton
First performed August 26, 1963

**36    PARTY MIX**
Music by Alexei Haieff
Costumes by Nancy Azara
Lighting by Thomas Skelton
First performed December 20, 1963

**37    THE RED ROOM**
Music by Gunther Schuller
Set and costumes by Alex Katz
First performed June 20, 1964

**38    DUET**
Music by Franz Josef Haydn
Costumes by George Tacet
Lighting by Thomas Skelton
First performed August 18, 1964

**39    FROM SEA TO SHINING SEA**
Music by Charles Ives (later by
    John Herbert McDowell*)
Costumes by John Rawlings
Lighting by Thomas Skelton
First performed March 31, 1965

**40    9 DANCES WITH MUSIC BY CORELLI**
Music by Arcangelo Corelli
Costumes by Rouben Ter-Arutunian
Lighting by William Ritman
First performed March 31, 1965

**41    POST MERIDIAN**
Music by Evelyn Lohoeffer de Boeck*
Costumes by Alex Katz
Lighting by Thomas Skelton
First performed March 31, 1965

**42    ORBS**
Music by Ludwig van Beethoven
Set and costumes by Alex Katz
Lighting by Jennifer Tipton
First performed July 4, 1966

43 AGATHE'S TALE
Music by Carlos Surinach*
Costumes by Julian Tomchin
Lighting by Jennifer Tipton
First performed August 12, 1967

44 LENTO
Music by Franz Josef Haydn
Costumes by George Tacet
Lighting by Jennifer Tipton
First performed August 12, 1967

45 PUBLIC DOMAIN
Music collage by John Herbert McDowell*
Costumes by John Rawlings
Lighting by Jennifer Tipton
First performed October 8, 1968

46 PRIVATE DOMAIN
Music by Iannis Xenakis
Set and costumes by Alex Katz
Lighting by Jennifer Tipton
First performed May 7, 1969

47 DUETS
Music by anonymous Medieval composers
Costumes by George Tacet
Lighting by Judith Daykin
First performed August 2, 1969

48 CHURCHYARD
Music by Cosmos Savage*
Costumes by Alec Sutherland
Lighting by Jennifer Tipton
First performed December 10, 1969

49 FOREIGN EXCHANGE
Music by Morton Subotnick
Set by Alex Katz
Costumes by Alec Sutherland
Lighting by Jennifer Tipton
First performed April 28, 1970

50 BIG BERTHA
Music from the St. Louis Melody Museum
    collection of band machines
Set and costumes by Alec Sutherland
Lighting by Jennifer Tipton
First performed November 6, 1970

51 BIG BERTHA
Duet version for television first aired
    March 1971

52 BOOK OF BEASTS
Music by Schubert, Weber, Saint-Saëns,
    Mozart, Beethoven, Boccherini, de Falla
    and Tchaikovsky, transcribed for harpsichord
Costumes by John Rawlings
Lighting by Jennifer Tipton
First performed July 2, 1971

53 FETES
Music by Claude Debussy
Costumes by George Tacet
Lighting by Jennifer Tipton
First performed October 16, 1971

54 GUESTS OF MAY
Music by Claude Debussy
Costumes by George Tacet
Lighting by Jennifer Tipton
First performed March 11, 1972

55 SO LONG EDEN
Music by John Fahey
Costumes by George Tacet
Lighting by Jennifer Tipton
First performed May 17, 1972
    (became part of the full-evening work,
    American Genesis)

56 NOAH'S MINSTRELS
Music by Louis Moreau Gottschalk
Set and costumes by George Tacet
Lighting by Jennifer Tipton
First performed February 17, 1973
    (became part of the full-evening work,
    American Genesis)

57 WEST OF EDEN
Music by Bohuslav Martinů
Costumes by George Tacet
Lighting by Jennifer Tipton
First performed October 13, 1973
    (was originally part of the full-evening work,
    American Genesis)

58 AMERICAN GENESIS
Music by Bach, Haydn, Fahey, Martinů and
    Gottschalk
Costumes by George Tacet
Lighting by Jennifer Tipton
First performed October 13, 1973

59 UNTITLED QUARTET
Music by Igor Stravinsky
Costumes by Rouben Ter-Arutunian
Lighting by Jennifer Tipton
First performed February 16, 1974
    (was a re-working of Fibers)

60 SPORTS AND FOLLIES
Music by Erik Satie
Costumes by George Tacet
Lighting by Jennifer Tipton
First performed August 7, 1974

61 ESPLANADE
Music by Johann Sebastian Bach
Costumes by John Rawlings
Lighting by Jennifer Tipton
First performed March 1, 1975

62 RUNES
Music by Gerald Busby*
Costumes by George Tacet
Lighting by Jennifer Tipton
First performed August 13, 1975

63 CLOVEN KINGDOM
Music by Arcangelo Corelli, Henry Cowell
    and Malloy Miller, combined by
    John Herbert McDowell
Women's costumes by Scott Barrie
Headpieces by John Rawlings
Lighting by Jennifer Tipton
First performed June 9, 1976

64 POLARIS
Music by Donald York*
Set and costumes by Alex Katz
Lighting by Jennifer Tipton
First performed August 26, 1976

65 IMAGES
Music by Claude Debussy
Costumes by Gene Moore
Lighting by Mark Litvin
First performed January 19, 1977

66 DUST
Music by Francis Poulenc
Set and costumes by Gene Moore
Lighting by Jennifer Tipton
First performed June 1, 1977

67 APHRODISIAMANIA
Renaissance music reorchestrated by
    Donald York
Scenario by Charles Ludlam
Set and costumes by Gene Moore
Lighting by Jennifer Tipton
First performed November 29, 1977

68 AIRS
Music by George Frideric Handel
Costumes by Gene Moore
Lighting by Jennifer Tipton
First performed May 30, 1978

69 DIGGITY
Music by Donald York*
Set and costumes by Alex Katz
Lighting by Mark Litvin
First performed November 3, 1978

70 NIGHTSHADE
Music by Alexander Scriabin
Costumes by Gene Moore
Lighting by Jennifer Tipton
First performed April 19, 1979

71 PROFILES
Music by Jan Radzynski*
Costumes by Gene Moore
Lighting by Mark Litvin
First performed July 28, 1979

72 LE SACRE DU PRINTEMPS
    (THE REHEARSAL)
Music by Igor Stravinsky
    (arrangement for piano)
Set and costumes by John Rawlings
Lighting by Jennifer Tipton
First performed January 15, 1980

73 ARDEN COURT
Music by William Boyce
Set and costumes by Gene Moore
Lighting by Jennifer Tipton
First performed April 15, 1981

74 HOUSE OF CARDS
Music by Darius Milhaud
Costumes by Cynthia O'Neal
Set by Mimi Gross
Lighting by Jennifer Tipton
First performed October 6, 1981

**75 LOST, FOUND AND LOST**
Elevator music reorchestrated by Donald York*
Costumes and stage design by Alex Katz
Lighting by Jennifer Tipton
First performed April 14, 1982

**76 MERCURIC TIDINGS**
Music by Franz Schubert
Costumes by Gene Moore
   (later by Santo Loquasto)
Lighting by Jennifer Tipton
First performed April 20, 1982

**77 MUSETTE**
Music by George Frideric Handel
Costumes by Gene Moore
Lighting by Jennifer Tipton
First performed April 5, 1983

**78 SUNSET**
Music by Edward Elgar
   (and recorded loon calls)
Set and costumes by Alex Katz
Lighting by Jennifer Tipton
First performed April 6, 1983

**79 SNOW WHITE**
Music by Donald York*
Set by David Gropman
Costumes by Cynthia O'Neal
Lighting by Jennifer Tipton
First performed April 13, 1983

**80 EQUINOX**
Music by Johannes Brahms
Costumes by William Ivey Long
Lighting by Jennifer Tipton
First performed December 1, 1983

**81 …BYZANTIUM**
Music by Edgard Varèse
Set by David Gropman
Costumes by William Ivey Long
Lighting by Jennifer Tipton
First performed March 20, 1984

**82 ROSES**
Music by Richard Wagner and
   Heinrich Baermann
Costumes by William Ivey Long
Lighting by Jennifer Tipton
First performed April 10, 1985

**83 LAST LOOK**
Music by Donald York*
Set and costumes by Alex Katz
Lighting by Jennifer Tipton
First performed April 16, 1985

**84 AB OVO USQUE AD MALA**
   **(FROM SOUP TO NUTS)**
Music by P.D.Q. Bach (Peter Schickele)
Set and costumes by Alex Katz
Lighting by Jennifer Tipton
First performed April 1, 1986

**85 MUSICAL OFFERING**
Music by Johann Sebastian Bach
   Orchestrations by Anton Webern and
   Frank Michael Beyer
Set and costumes by Gene Moore
Lighting by Jennifer Tipton
First performed April 8, 1986

**86 SYZYGY**
Music by Donald York*
Costumes by Gene Moore
   (later by Santo Loquasto)
Lighting by Jennifer Tipton
First performed April 21, 1987

**87 KITH AND KIN**
Music by Wolfgang Amadeus Mozart
Costumes by William Ivey Long
Lighting by Jennifer Tipton
First performed April 28, 1987

**88 BRANDENBURGS**
Music by Johann Sebastian Bach
Costumes by William Ivey Long
   (later by Santo Loquasto)
Lighting by Jennifer Tipton
First performed April 5, 1988

**89 COUNTERSWARM**
Music by György Ligeti
Costumes by Santo Loquasto
Lighting by Jennifer Tipton
First performed April 28, 1988

**90 DANBURY MIX**
Music by Charles Ives
Set by David Gropman
Costumes by William Ivey Long
Lighting by Jennifer Tipton
First performed May 12, 1988

**91 SPEAKING IN TONGUES**
Music by Matthew Patton
Set and costumes by Santo Loquasto
Lighting by Jennifer Tipton
First performed November 10, 1988

**92 MINIKIN FAIR**
Music by David Koblitz, Douglas Wieselman
   and Thaddeus Spae
Set and costumes by Santo Loquasto
Lighting by Jennifer Tipton
First performed April 15, 1989

**93 THE SORCERER'S SOFA**
Music by Paul Dukas
Set and costumes by Santo Loquasto
Lighting by Jennifer Tipton
First performed November 2, 1989

**94 OF BRIGHT & BLUE BIRDS &**
**THE GALA SUN**
Music by Donald York*
Set and costumes by Santo Loquasto
Lighting by Jennifer Tipton
First performed April 25, 1990

**95 FACT AND FANCY (3 EPITAPHS & ALL)**
Early New Orleans jazz, and reggae
Costumes by Robert Rauschenberg
   (3 Epitaphs) and George Tacet
Lighting by Jennifer Tipton
First performed June 6, 1991

**96 COMPANY B**
Songs sung by the Andrews Sisters
Costumes by Santo Loquasto
Lighting by Jennifer Tipton
First performed June 20, 1991

**97 SPEAKING IN TONGUES**
Version for television first aired
   September 26, 1991

**98 OZ**
Music by Wayne Horvitz and Robin Holcomb
Set and costumes by Santo Loquasto
Lighting by Jennifer Tipton
First performed in 1991

**99 SPINDRIFT**
Music by Arnold Schoenberg
Set and costumes by Santo Loquasto
Lighting by Jennifer Tipton
First performed July 8, 1993

**100 A FIELD OF GRASS**
Songs sung by Harry Nilsson
Costumes by Santo Loquasto
Lighting by Jennifer Tipton
First performed October 27, 1993

**101 FUNNY PAPERS**
Music: novelty tunes
Choreography of Sandra Stone, Mary
   Cochran, Hernando Cortez, David Grenke,
   Andrew Asnes and Patrick Corbin
Amended and combined by Paul Taylor
Costumes by Santo Loquasto
Lighting by Jennifer Tipton
First performed October 12, 1994

**102 MOONBINE**
Music by Claude Debussy
Costumes by Santo Loquasto
Lighting by Jennifer Tipton
First performed October 13, 1994

**103 OFFENBACH OVERTURES**
Music by Jacques Offenbach
Costumes by Santo Loquasto
Lighting by Jennifer Tipton
First performed October 12, 1995

**104 PRIME NUMBERS**
Music by David Israel
Costumes by Santo Loquasto
Lighting by Jennifer Tipton
First performed January 10, 1997

**105 EVENTIDE**
Music by Ralph Vaughan Williams
Set and costumes by Santo Loquasto
Lighting by Jennifer Tipton
First performed February 25, 1997

**106 PIAZZOLLA CALDERA**
Music by Astor Piazzolla and
   Jerzy Peterburshsky
Set and costumes by Santo Loquasto
Lighting by Jennifer Tipton
First performed June 12, 1997

**107 THE WORD**
Music by David Israel*
Costumes by Santo Loquasto
Lighting by Jennifer Tipton
First performed March 4, 1998

**108  FIDDLERS GREEN**
Music by John Adams
Costumes by Santo Loquasto
Lighting by Jennifer Tipton
First performed May 23, 1998

**109  OH, YOU KID!**
Ragtime music (performed by the Paragon
    Ragtime Orchestra)
Set and costumes by Santo Loquasto
Lighting by Jennifer Tipton
First performed February 18, 1999

**110  CASCADE**
Music by Johann Sebastian Bach
Costumes by Santo Loquasto
Lighting by Jennifer Tipton
First performed July 22, 1999

**111  ARABESQUE**
Music by Claude Debussy
Costumes by Santo Loquasto
Lighting by Jennifer Tipton
First performed October 15, 1999

**112  FIENDS ANGELICAL**
Music by George Crumb
Set and costumes by Santo Loquasto
Lighting by Jennifer Tipton
First performed July 25, 2000

**113  DANDELION WINE**
Music by Pietro Locatelli
Costumes by Santo Loquasto
Lighting by Jennifer Tipton
First performed November 16, 2000

**114  BLACK TUESDAY**
Songs from the Great Depression
Sets and costumes by Santo Loquasto
Lighting by Jennifer Tipton
First performed April 10, 2001

**115  ANTIQUE VALENTINE**
Music by Johann Sebastian Bach, Weber, Haydn,
    Beethoven, Chopin and Mendelssohn played
    on music boxes, player piano, and mechanical
    organ
Costumes by Santo Loquasto
Lighting by Jennifer Tipton
First performed October 26, 2001

**116  PROMETHEAN FIRE**
Music by Johann Sebastian Bach, transcribed by
    Leopold Stokowski
Set and costumes by Santo Loquasto
Lighting by Jennifer Tipton
First performed June 6, 2002

**117  DREAM GIRLS**
Barbershop quartet songs sung by
    The Buffalo Bills
Set and costumes by Santo Loquasto
Lighting by Jennifer Tipton
First performed October 18, 2002

**118  IN THE BEGINNING**
Music by Carl Orff
    Orchestrated by Friedrich K. Wanek
Sets and costumes by Santo Loquasto
Lighting by Jennifer Tipton
First performed April 9, 2003

**119  LE GRAND PUPPETIER**
Music by Igor Stravinsky
    Played on pianola
Set and costumes by Santo Loquasto
Lighting by Jennifer Tipton
First performed March 2, 2004

**120  DANTE VARIATIONS**
Music by György Ligeti
Set and costumes by Santo Loquasto
Lighting by Jennifer Tipton
First performed March 24, 2004

**121  KLEZMERBLUEGRASS**
Traditional Klezmer and Bluegrass music
Arranged by Margot Leverett
Costumes by Santo Loquasto
Lighting by Jennifer Tipton
First performed October 24, 2004

**122  SPRING ROUNDS**
Music by Richard Strauss
    (after François Couperin)
Costumes by Santo Loquasto
Lighting by Jennifer Tipton
First performed July 5, 2005

**123  BANQUET OF VULTURES**
Music by Morton Feldman
Costumes by Santo Loquasto
Lighting by Jennifer Tipton
First performed October 29, 2005

**124  TROILUS AND CRESSIDA (REDUCED)**
Music by Amilcare Ponchielli
Costumes by Santo Loquasto
Lighting by Jennifer Tipton
First performed April 15, 2006

**125  LINES OF LOSS**
Music by Guillaume de Machaut,
    Christopher Tye, Jack Body, John Cage,
    Arvo Pärt and Alfred Schnittke
Costumes by Santo Loquasto
Lighting by Jennifer Tipton
First performed March 2, 2007

**126  DE SUEÑOS (OF DREAMS)**
Music by Agustín Lara, Juan García Esquivel,
    Osvaldo Golijov, B. García de Jesús, J. Elizondo,
    Ariel Guzik, and Chalino Sánchez
Set and costumes by Santo Loquasto
Lighting by Jennifer Tipton
First performed July 12, 2007

**127  DE SUEÑOS QUE SE REPITEN**
      **(OF RECURRING DREAMS)**
Music by Ariel Guzik, Silvestre Revueltas,
    Margarita Lecuona, Robert Gómez Bolaños,
    and Severiano Briseño
Set and costumes by Santo Loquasto
Lighting by Jennifer Tipton
First performed November 2, 2007

**128  CHANGES**
Songs sung by The Mamas & The Papas
Costumes by Santo Loquasto
Lighting by Jennifer Tipton
First performed April 22, 2008

**129  BELOVED RENEGADE**
Music by Francis Poulenc
Costumes by Santo Loquasto
Lighting by Jennifer Tipton
First performed November 21, 2008

**130  ALSO PLAYING**
Music by Gaetano Donizetti
Costumes by Santo Loquasto
Lighting by Jennifer Tipton
First performed April 8, 2009

**131  BRIEF ENCOUNTERS**
Music by Claude Debussy
Costumes by Santo Loquasto
Lighting by James F. Ingalls
First performed November 6, 2009

**132  PHANTASMAGORIA**
Music by anonymous Renaissance composers
Costumes by Santo Loquasto
Lighting by Jennifer Tipton
First performed July 15, 2010

**133  THREE DUBIOUS MEMORIES**
Music by Peter Elyakim Taussig
Costumes by Santo Loquasto
Lighting by Jennifer Tipton
First performed October 30, 2010

**134  THE UNCOMMITTED**
Music by Arvo Pärt
Set and costumes by Santo Loquasto
Lighting by Jennifer Tipton
First performed July 21, 2011

**135  GOSSAMER GALLANTS**
Music by Bedřich Smetana
Set and costumes by Santo Loquasto
Lighting by Jennifer Tipton
First performed November 19, 2011

**136  HOUSE OF JOY**
Music by Donald York*
Set and costumes by Santo Loquasto
Lighting by Jennifer Tipton
First performed March 17, 2012

**137  TO MAKE CROPS GROW**
Music by Ferde Grofé
Costumes by Santo Loquasto
Lighting by James F. Ingalls
First performed November 3, 2012

**138  PERPETUAL DAWN**
Music by Johann David Heinichen
Set and costumes by Santo Loquasto
Lighting by James F. Ingalls
First performed March 5, 2013

**139  AMERICAN DREAMER**
Music by Stephen Foster
Songs sung by Thomas Hampson
Set and costumes by Santo Loquasto
Lighting by Jennifer Tipton
First performed August 5, 2013

**140  MARATHON CADENZAS**
Music by Raymond Scott
Set and costumes by Santo Loquasto
Lighting by James F. Ingalls
First performance: March 14, 2014

# PAUL TAYLOR DANCE FOUNDATION

STAFF
Artistic Director: Paul Taylor
Rehearsal Director: Bettie de Jong
Paul Taylor 2 Dance Company Rehearsal Director: Ruth Andrien
Taylor School Director: Raegan Wood
Assisant to the Artistic Director: Andy LeBeau
Assisant to the Rehearsal Director: Michael Trusnovec

Principal Lighting Designer: Jennifer Tipton
Principal Set & Costume Designer: Santo Loquasto

Executive Director: John Tomlinson
Director of Development: Daniel Vincent
Director of Marketing and Communications: Alan Olshan
Director of Finance: Sarah Schindler
Company Manager: Holden Kellerhals
Director of Public Relations: Lisa Labrado
Director of Tour Engagements: Tim Robinson
Administrator and Archival Supervisor: Tom Patrick
Development Officer: Nora Webb
Development Assistant: Catherine Hong
Assistant to the Executive Director: Laura Alexander

Production and Assistant Company Manager: Steven Carlino
Production Manager, Taylor 2: Bridget Welty
Lighting Supervisor: Michael Dostal
Wardrobe Supervisor: Clarion Overmoyer

Information Technology Consultant: Andy LeBeau, PC Umbrella
International Tour Booking: Jane Hermann, JPH Consultants
Taylor 2 Tour Booking: Jeannette Gardner, Gardner Arts Network
Archival Consultant: Linda Edgerly, The Winthrop Group
Auditor: Michael Wallace, Lutz & Carr
Orthopedic Specialist: David S. Weiss, M.D.
Travel Agent: Michael Retsina, Altour

PAUL TAYLOR DANCE COMPANY: THE DIAMOND ANNIVERSARY
Edited by Alan Olshan
Designed by Andrew Jerabek
Archival research by Tom Patrick and Angela Kane, Ph.D.
Interns: Andrea Ellis, Brittany Greene, Nicole McLaughlin

PHOTO CREDITS
Tom Caravaglia: pages 7, 29, 55, 62, 63, 67-69
Dennis Deloria: page 17
Paul B. Goode: pages 6, 8, 12, 16, 19, 21-24, 27, 28, 30-33, 35-49, 51-54, 56, 57, 59, 61, 64-66, 70, 71, front flap
© Lois Greenfield: pages 3, 5, 11, 50, 58, 60
Jack Mitchell: pages 2, 14, 18, 20, 25, 26, 72
William Schipp: page 15
© 1978, 1980 Jack Vartoogian/FrontRowPhotos: pages 34, 10